MILDENHALL
FEN TIGERS
(1992-20

GW00746267

ROY BRAZ~~~
© 2013

VOL: TWO
THE RECORD YEARS

ISBN 978-0-9536518-4-9

First Edition June 2013

Published by

ROMARY BOOKS
01440 714877

INTRODUCTION

Part two of the Mildenhall Fen Tigers history sees a spell in the early 1990's, when the sound of speedway bikes at West Row Stadium was absent for some prolonged periods. However, they were eventually re-born to take their place once again in British Speedway, operating in the lower league, and through its several name changes. Entering the Twenty-First Century in due course brought some more success in league and cup, before a grievous three-year spell in the Premier League, and setting an unwanted record in the process in their third season in the middle tier of British Speedway. Back to the third level and the main reason why Mildenhall Speedway was originally formed; still giving youngsters a chance to make a name in the sport. The Fen Tigers, guided by a promotion team who have Mildenhall at heart set a record in 2012 which will be very hard to equal, and with probably the youngest team in the league.

****

ACKNOWLEDGEMENTS
Derek Leader (illustrations); Tony Turner (design of front cover); Alan Hardy (screening); Cambridge News; Mildenhall Speedway; Speedway Star; plus the invaluable help of Jason Gardner for history facts. This book is also dedicated to Brian and my group of friends who each meeting share the same spot on the first bend.

<u>1992</u>

While missing out in the 1991 season a new Mildenhall promoter Dick Partridge was busy with his aspirations of getting speedway operating at West Row once again. First, there was the introduction of Greyhound Racing at the stadium, optimistically bringing in some of the extra cash to enable the speedway to be staged as well. The venue itself was then given a makeover after a few years looking a bit dreary. Derek Hewitt who had ridden a few second-half's at the old Firs at Norwich, then climbed aboard the Fen Tigers train and an application was put to the BSPA as late as January 1992 and they were granted the licence to bring back the sound of bikes in top action at Mildenhall, and to the speedway world once more. It had helped the ruling body out of a hole when Swindon were to be relegated from the top league, but said they would rather close down altogether than drop to Division Two, so with the Fen Tigers back in the fold both Division's had the equal number of clubs.

The two year enforced break with no Mildenhall Speedway team functioning riding, gave them a breather and a chance to step back, recover their breath, and look at what had been achieved since the humble beginnings of a fenland field almost in the middle of nowhere. Ipswich's John Louis took advantage during the winter to run a Polish Training School at the West Row track. However, it was not the time for the Fen Tigers to rest on their laurels, as there was a team to put together. The only difference was the now smaller track at 285 metres which was now inside the greyhound track at West Row, the new layout being the work mainly of Jeremy Doncaster, and which together with stock cars had made the compact stadium into a multi-sport venue. The fence for the speedway track was now of a chain-link type, which was thought to be much safer than the original, boarded one. Other improvements were better lighting and a comprehensible public address system plus concrete steps on the first and second bends. Already the club had attracted some sponsors including Edmonds Transport who arranged the first load of shale from Huddersfield without charge, and Brian's Circuit Tractors provided a tractor and other machinery. Also free of charge the printers 'Keyprint' had produced a brochure outlining all the options that were available in sponsoring the Fen Tigers. For those who wanted to make a proper day out the Speedway Restaurant advertised its opening at lunch-time for a three-course roast lunch for only £5-50.

The new bosses Partridge and Hewitt had assembled a team for the start of the 1992 season in the third tier of British speedway, now called the British League Division Two, and sponsored by Homefire. The line-up included Jamie Habbin, Gary Tagg, Nigel Leaver, David Smart, Savalas Clouting and local hero Mel Taylor who was returning to his home track after some time away since 1989 when he left for Rye House. He had never got used to their track and had tried to get away for three years until returning to his original club; he was also the fresh captain. Savalas Clouting was listed as a Mildenhall rider and completed in the opening meeting as a Fen Tiger, but never actually rode an official match for the team, all down to the laws of averages, but later he got his chance with Ipswich. He made the switch to Arena Essex in May after early season spells with Ipswich and Poole.

Nigel Leaver from the Midlands joined Mildenhall in the winter from Kings Lynn, having started his career with Cradley Heath, and he had ridden for Arena Essex, Belle Vue, Wimbledon and Long Eaton. Jamie Habbin was another ex Fen Tiger to return home (nicknamed the Pink Panther on account of his colourful leathers) after a spell with Newcastle in 1991. Before that with Long Eaton (1990). His career started at Peterborough in 1986 before joining Fen Tigers in 1989; he had won both the Anglia and British rider's championship when with Kings Lynn. Ian Barney was on a month's loan from Milton Keynes after beginning his riding at Peterborough in 1980, moving to Exeter (1990).and joining Sheffield in 1991. He was a former Second Division champion in1984. Gary Tagg started his career with Milton Keynes in 1985 and had spells with Eastbourne, Reading, Hackney and Peterborough before going back to the Knights in mid season (1991). David Smart had been with Exeter in 1991 after Swindon in 1990 and again in 1992 and came to the Fen Tigers on loan from Swindon. Jesper Olsen came in later to strengthen the tale end of the team. Olsen was a former Amateur champions in Denmark, and had some rides with Wimbledon and was bought from Eastbourne where he had spent his first year riding in British speedway. He said he liked the atmosphere and the track at Mildenhall. Mel Taylor was returning to his original club after being with British League teams, mainly Kings Lynn and Oxford.

The re-opening meeting at West Row on 22 March was a grand individual contest for the Auto Valet Trophy, which attracted a crowd of 1,500. There was an interesting list of competitors which included two future world champions; Tony Rickardsson who was with Ipswich then, Chris Louis, and Billy Hamill of Cradley Heath. Other star names included Amando Castagno (Reading), Sean Wilson (Bradford), Alan Grahame (Stoke) and Jeremy Doncaster (Reading). Rickardsson was the top dog and rode a flawless fifteen-point maximum in winning all his heats, with Hamill one point behind. Of the new Mildenhall seven, only Jamie Habbin managed to win a heat with David Smart registering four second places. There had been rain in the morning and during the meeting itself but the meeting went ahead, although the track was far from perfect, and it was due to the immense efforts of Robert 'Huggie' Huggins and his gang that racing was possible. After an episode of falls, the referee spoke to all the riders who all wanted to carry on for the large crowds' sake, which had gathered for the first meeting at West Row for a long time, and they made light of the increasing conditions and everyone went home happy.

After losing their opening two home fixtures, to Swedish touring side Rospiggarna 47-43 and then Peterborough in the Gold Cup 42-38, the new Fen Tigers were considered mere cannon fodder and were written off by many pundits. In the Peterborough side at West Row was a young 16-year-old 'Wonder Boy' Jason Crump, another future World Champions to appear there. On this appearance, he managed two plus a bonus riding at number six. However, the so-called experts forgot about the determination of the Suffolk side and surprised everyone when they downed the Peterborough colours in the Cup, and took their unbeaten record from them on their County Showground track 47-43. Both teams were not at all happy with the referee keeping them longer than usual at the starting gate. Both captains complained and one rider burnt out two clutches, while another seized up an engine. In the Peterborough victory, Nigel Leaver and David Smart went very well while Olsen

-3-

showed up well.

In the International match against the Sweden side the Tigers Cubs were also in action for the first time in the season, meeting a side named the Scorcerers Apprentices, who comprised of Lawrence Hare, Gary Wells, Jason Wilby and a very young Shaun Tacey from nearby Norwich. The Cubs team was Savalas Clouting, Nathan Wilson, Jason Gage and Clive Clark. The same foursome had another outing in the meeting with Peterborough who called their youngsters the Thundercats. Several people were of the opinion that the new shorter track would not be as exciting but were soon convinced after the new circuit racing was as good, if not better.

On Sunday 11 April, the Tigers turned over a Long Eaton team who included the two Blackbird boys Carl and Paul, ex-Tigers, at home by 47-43 but skipper Mel Taylor bruised his hand in a crash. He was in the Stoke meeting of the Qualifying World Championship and after two pointless rides, he changed his gearing and finished with three second places. At the Long Eaton meeting, the Tigers Cubs were in action for the third time against Nottingham Archers and Adrian Mountain came into the Cubs line-up. On 18 April away at Stoke, the team was as in first meeting, with the exception of Mikael TuernbergI who came in for Clouting and at reserve Jesper Olsen. Tuernberg was making his debut after impressing for the touring side when they visited West Row, and had quickly signed a contract and applied for a work permit. Swedish born Mikael was reckoned to be the next top rider from that country and soon began massing the points for Mildenhall.

Rye House and Exeter were both beaten in turn when they came calling at the Fen Tigers Den, but the Mildenhall team were proving bad travellers and dropped the points at Rye House and Exeter. An incident at Rye House saw Gary Tagg banned for three matches for 'withholding his services' a term which did not tell all. He arrived early at Rye House with his mechanic and when Mildenhall's Dick Partridge turned up the Rye House management told him that due to a falling out between Gary's mechanic and Ronnie Russell's family, they would not allow the mechanic in the stadium. Tagg took a stand with his mechanic and the Tigers rode one short. Jason Gage took his place in the team for the few

-4-

next fixtures; Gary had also incurred a fine for missing the Rye House match. When Milton Keynes Knights arrived at West Row on 3 May, they were seen to include Ian Barney who had suddenly left the Tigers and was said to be returning to Peterborough. The Knights were beaten 49-41 with Nigel Weaver top scoring with 12 points. This Sunday saw a new competition for the Tigers Cubs when they were up against Milton Keynes youngsters in what was billed as the Division Two Reserve Gold Cup; quite a mouthful. This meeting kicked off three hours later so supporters who wished could take in the British semi-final at Ipswich early in the day. Off the track, a meeting was held at West Row Stadium to form an official Supporters Club, which drew a large attendance.

On Wednesday 6 May, Mildenhall were away at Long Eaton in the Division Two Gold Cup (2nd leg). Riding for the homesters were Carl and Paul Blackbird ex Mildenhall In this match there was also a Reserve League match Nottingham Archers v Mildenhall Fen Tiger Cubs who were represented by Adrian Mountain, Jason Gage, Clive Clark and Nathan Wilson. In their programme notes, Long Eaton said that West Row was the best stadium in the lower leagues and always a pleasant and compact place to visit.

One of the top British Speedway teams were the opposition for Mildenhall in the newly created BSPA Cup when lower teams were each drawn against one of the big boys, and Oxford Cheetahs were at Mildenhall on 10 May. It was also the time to launch a brand new-look programme, the ones so far for 1992 had been rather drab and there were many complaints. Jesper Olsen was away on the World Championship trail and Tagg came back into the team after settling his differences with the Tigers. Leading Oxford was top rider Hans Nielsen, who had appeared in the last twelve World Championship finals, being champion three times and runner-up in another three; who swept to an imposing fifteen-point maximum, breaking the track record (50.9) in his first heat. Mildenhall were on the wrong end of a 54-36 defeat, but this was to be expected unless the most unusual things happened to change the course of the meeting. Last image of the meeting was Hans Nielson leaning over the safety fence on the back straight, busy signing autographs well after the end of racing; now that's class. The Tiger Cubs took on an Oxford Select in this meeting as well, and so were not left

-5-

out of a top meeting.

The next visitors to West Row in the Gold Cup were the Stoke Potters who were a formidable side and were one of the favourites to win the League, this they showed inflicting a 51-39 defeat on Mildenhall, who raced this meeting on a Monday evening, a most unusual day of the week for a Fen Tigers home meeting. In the Stoke line-up was former Tigers favourite Eric Monaghan who was at Mildenhall for three seasons, and who showed he still likes the track with three straight wins for his new team. Olsen missed the match for the Tigers as he was hospitalised after a crash at Stangerup the previous week with broken ribs; he was soon back in this country and wanted to ride again as quickly as possible but he had to miss the next few weeks. The referee for the Stoke meeting Frank Ebdon took time out to congratulate the Fen Tigers 'Huggy' for the excellent track saying it was "a breath of fresh air" to see such a well prepared racing strip.

A few weeks later in an Inter-League Challenge, Mildenhall came face-to-face with fellow Suffolk side Ipswich but could not rise to the occasion and went under 51-39. Two more Mildenhall riders from the past turned up in the Long Eaton Invaders team in the Homefire Division Two fixture on 24 May. Carl Blackbird rattled up fourteen points on his return but could not prevent the visitors from going down 48-39. Brother Paul was not so fruitful registering a blank return. The meeting versus Glasgow proved a tight affair ending at forty-five points to each side, and this after Mildenhall were eight points ahead with two heats to go.

Losing heavily away but winning the home meetings were seen to be Mildenhall's fortunes as the season progressed. The meetings at Berwick and Exeter were both very bad, and also on two very wet tracks that these matches were rode, and of course there was no passing at all once out the gate. Nigel Leaver broke down on his way north and missed the Berwick encounter while Olsen crashed heavily and only took two races. 68-22 being the final score. At Exeter, it was just as wet and mud made proper racing impossible. Mel Taylor crashed when his engine blew up and he took no further part in the meeting while two other riders were struggling with injuries. A dreadful score of 71-19 was the Tigers lot, with nobody reaching double figures, as they made a miserable way home to East Anglia. The team manager did not blame anyone for not trying; indeed, he praised all the team for making a great effort on the two nights in question.

A first time visit to West Row by Sheffield was on 7 June, a club who had like the Fen Tigers, suffered a two-year shutdown, before re-appearing in the Second Division, but were really struggling to make ends meet at this time, and crowds of around one thousand were well below the minimum needed to survive. The promoters were in the act of selling out to another company to see if they could stop the financial rot. Mildenhall added to their woe with a 52-37 victory as the Tigers fielded a full strength line-up for a change. When two of their riders not turning up Sheffield borrowed young Jason Gage to make up their team, scoring one point.

The writing was also on the wall for Mildenhall as well and the accomplished success on the track at home was drawing well under the break-even figure of nine hundred at each home meeting. This together with co-promoter Derek Hewitt quitting the partnership with Dick Partridge did not bode well, even the greyhound racing crowds had dropped by a large margin. On the track, the away meeting at Peterborough was rained-off and the Tigers travelled to Exeter to come bottom of the pile in the first of the Four-Team Tournament with fifteen points. The sudden closure of the Milton Keynes track meant no Four-Team meeting at home for them and the third leg was a West Row on 17 June. Mildenhall, for the first time came second in their home meeting in the Four-Team tussle, scoring 26 to Rye House 30; Milton Keynes got 23 and Exeter 17. Starting after this meeting was a Free Disco after the meeting at 7-30 and after each Sunday, "too good to miss" was the blurb.

The Fen Tigers had looked all ready for the new season and had opened with a new enthusiasm and the supporters were still eager to see them racing once again. However, with no real indication in the latest programme, it all came to a sudden halt at the end of June after just four meetings in the league, three at home, and the club folded once again. This after they had won their two League home meetings. To be truthful the promoters had warned in the programme notes for some time that the attendances were falling well below that expected to keep running, The Promoters lost quite a bit of money in trying to keep the Fen Tigers active but there were not enough spectators coming through the turnstiles to make it worthwhile. Six hundred people watched the final meeting of 1992. Graham Edmonds, a former rider with Kings Lynn came in to try a rescue mission, which unfortunately did not get anywhere, and Mildenhall officially closed down on 3 July 1992. This brought another two summers with no Fen Tigers in Sunday afternoon action.

****

1994

The club were re-launched yet again with high hopes this was not another false dawn, after being in the wilderness after their mid-season collapse of 1992. They were also competing in the brand new British League Division Three formed it was said to try and provide a stepping stone for the younger riders just entering the sport. Forgetting the sudden halt in 1992, the Fen Tigers had ridden 523 meetings since they were formed in 1975 and their average position in the League over those years was a presentable eighth place. After many fans expressed their desire to see the Fen Tigers back in action, former short term promoter Derek Hewitt took control once again with Dingle Brown an ex-Rayleigh rider joining as the team manager while one of the favourite Tigers of the past, Robert Henry took the post of machine examiner. Early July was pencilled in as the start of this season as there were only six teams taking part in the new league; Berwick, Buxton, Iwade, Linlithgow and Stoke, together with Mildenhall.

Amongst their better publicity, the Fen Tigers put on a trial for riders who wished to ride in the coming season, and a host of riders arrived all looking perky and ready. Ex Arena Essex star, Simon Wolstenholme and former Rye House Martin Cobbin were the pick of the bunch. There had been twenty-seven mainly hopefuls on 10 July trying to catch the eye of the new promotion and six were selected to form the team for the opening fixture, and with number seven undecided it was left to start the opening meeting with a special race to determine who takes the seven colours. Steve Battle was the one to come out of this race and took his place in the team. A newly programmed rider named Adrian

-8-

Thompson did not in fact ride for Mildenhall, Steve Knott taking his place, and Thompson did not appear in the team at all in 1994. Another well-known face coming into the Tigers set-up was Malcolm Vasey as Presenter and programme editor.

There was a good attendance which saw local hero Michael Lee officially declare the track open once again. The Fen Tigers entertained Iwade (Sittingbourne) in the opening meeting, although they took the title of Kent Crusaders with memories of the Canterbury Crusaders of the past. Over one thousand spectators had flocked to the Iwade track for their very first meeting after many years as a training track only. Although the visitors provided the most heat winners Mildenhall came out on top 41-37 after being in front from the second heat onwards. The Fen Tigers seven were Simon Wolstenholmel (10+1), Peter Boast (4+1), Martin Cobbin (5), Gary Sweet (4+2), Steve Knott (9), Sid Cooper (2+1) and Steve Battle (7+1). However, it was Sittingbourne's Kevin Teager who rode a twelve-point maximum, but the best thing of the afternoon was that speedway and Mildenhall were back in operation once again.

The Fen Tigers then went on their travels to the distant North of the British Isles to take on Berwick and suffered their first loss by 48-27, with Gary Sweet top scoring with eight. It was then on to face Linlithgow Lightning, the first new club in Scotland for twenty years, and this provided the Tigers with another heavy defeat 52-26 and this time top scorer was Martin Cobbin who amassed nine points. Over the years, the annual trek to Scotland was never a very fruitful journey for Mildenhall. Members of the promotion team and staff were not averse to putting their hands in their pockets to help financially and for the Northern Tour it was Mr Vasey who helped with the cost of lodgings for the riders for their night away from home. The promotion did however appeal for anyone who had a tin, or even a half tin, of white paint to perk up the safety fence and white line painting.

For their second home meeting, and a later than usual start of 7-30pm, Linlithgow were the visitors to West Row for the return fixture, and Carl Johnson came into the home side in place of Steve Knott. This proved a tight match won by Mildenhall 40-38. For the Scottish team a certain

Geoff Powell was back on a bike after having a break from the sport, and registering eleven points as well as winning the second half final. At that time there were full second half races known by various different names; The Fen Flyer being the favourite this new season. This also saw more young riders having a ride in Opportunity Races, and the Reserves Revenge.

Regrettably the enthusiasm of the Iwade club had quickly faded and it was sad when they announced they were closing to league racing, so next up at West Row were the Cleveland Bays who had come into Division Three to take the place of the Kent club. The Bays operated from Cleveland Park, the home of Middlesborough Bears and amongst their riders were Stuart and Jonathan Swales the sons of BSPA Chairman Tim Swales. Mildenhall's Simon Wolstenholme gained a twelve-point maximum in their 41-37 victory.

There looked like there was to be a prodigious competition for places in the Fen Tigers team, and one who was beginning to improve and stake a claim was young Dean Garrod with some bright second half rides. Then there was 21 year-old Mark Wilkinson who travelled up from Redruth in Cornwall to try his luck in the second half's at West Row. This youngster had experienced very limited opportunity's elsewhere and came to the Fen Tigers who welcomed him and gave him his chance in the second-half's which is what Mildenhall is all about.

Berwick Bandits arrived at Mildenhall with an unbeaten record and manage to hang on to this as another very close match saw the Tigers go down 41-37. Berwick were another club like Mildenhall with a remote track away from the town at Berrington Lough and were also in the process of trying to re-establish speedway in the Border country. A win in their next home meeting by Mildenhall over Buxton Hitmen by 46-29, the biggest margin of victory so far. The Derbyshire club were one of the newest in the country and were managed by former England international Chris Morton. The previous Saturday these two teams were due to meet at Buxton but the weather intervened to stop the action. The fixture list was being re-arranged and resulted in Mildenhall having to travel to the Hitmen on 24 September, just two days after a trip to Cleveland; this tested the resolve of the young riders coming into the sport at the time and to keep the bikes up to standard, as well as their own toughness and professionalism. The match at Cleveland saw a change in the Mildenhall line-up when Tony Kingsbury made his debut, taking over from Sid Cooper, and then Carl Johnson was replaced by Dean Garrod who appeared for the first time in the away meeting at Buxton starting with a healthy seven points.

Up to this time in the new season, there had been no official supporters club and plans were put into action to see one formed to be a key role in keeping the Fen Tigers in operation. The management had arranged a 'Shindig' evening on 26 November (Saturday) a Social event with Video's, Quizzes, and other entertainment to celebrate the Tigers first season back in harness; the riders were also expected to be in attendance.

The Fen Tigers captain Simon Wolstenholme suffered a broken shoulder and bruised lungs after a crash at Long Eaton in the Division Three Riders Championship. This was in the first heat of that evening and Simon missed the end of the season. The Tigers other representative Gary Sweet lost his chance when he blew an engine during the meeting. Wolstenholme set an example to all the other riders when he turned up to cheer the lads on at Stoke and at West Row. Stoke Potters then arrived at West Row after having a similar amount of time on the sidelines as Mildenhall but were making a comeback into the speedway world. Owing to a big printing error, the visitors were given the name of Buxton in the days programme. Stoke had beaten the Tigers the night before at Loomer Road by 51-25. For the home encounter match Steve Knott was promoted to the number one spot and Darren Andrews at number two, an entirely new pairing at the top end of the team. Unfortunately, it was not the Tigers day and they lost their second home defeat 39-37 after being in the lead until the last heat. At his new position, Knott produced a twelve-point maximum. He had not (*no pun intended*) been in the Tigers line-up since the first meeting and one wonders where he had been all season.

The 1994 season ended with a home meeting that saw a Peterborough Select side take on Mildenhall, bringing back memories of these two foes facing each other in many meetings over the years. The visitors included Carl Johnson and Darren Andrews in their team and a stirring match ending at Mildenhall 39 Peterborough 38. Although Mildenhall finished fifth out of six teams it was still deemed a successful season albeit a short one, but the training schools were continuing all through the winter months at West Row and the promoters looked back on a job well done. The attendances averaged out around seven hundred, which was a break-even total, and Derek Hewitt summed it up "We are very lucky at Mildenhall with the supporters and the promoter's right behind the club, and the ambition is still here." The Fen Tigers were back to stay.

****

1995

There were some changes in the set up of the major leagues for the new season which saw a combination of all the previous years First Division teams with nine of the Second Division, making a strong Premier League, and as part of this the Third Division was re-named the British Speedway Academy League. From the previous season, all the teams returned while Sittingbourne, formerly Iwade came back into the fold together with new team Exeter known as the Devon Demons. This strengthened the look of the league and gave four more matches. With speedway the hardest sport in which to make a breakthrough into there were at least ten young riders who looked the part in training for the new season at West Row, and there seemed to be a fight for team places again.

The opening meeting however was the prestigious British Under 21 Championship (Qualifying Round, which was a feather in the Mildenhall hat as the Speedway bosses recognised the way the Fen Tigers had fought back after a spell of not operating. Amongst the sixteen young riders were two names for the future Ipswich's Scott Nichollls and Andre Compton. Rain spoilt the opening heats but the track staff worked wonders to get it in better condition when it stopped and the meeting went off well. In front of a one thousand crowd, the winner on the day turned out to be Justin Elkins of Poole with three first places and two seconds, runner-up was Steve Knott the Mildenhall rider and third Scott Nicholls. Another Fen Tiger in the meeting was Steve Battle, memorable for his long flowing hair and his exciting leg-trailing style, who did not have a good meeting scoring just four points. This event had been ongoing since 1969 and its list of previous winners included Peter Collins, Michael Lee, Kenny Carter, Carl Blackbird and Mark Loram.

Mildenhall set themselves up for the new campaign with a challenge over two legs with the reigning Division Three champions Berwick, naming it the Fen/Tweed Trophy. For the home leg and the first meeting at West Row, the Fen Tigers reverted to the previous season's race-off to fill the number seven race jacket, and as before Steve Battle took his place in the final line-up. Most of last years riders were back with just one newcomer for the start, this being Andy Giddings Berwick came out on top 56-40.and Mildenhall then knew what they were up against the coming season.

It was interesting at this stage of the new Tigers that it was inevitable that changes would be made to the line-up each season as some riders sought pastures new or looked for a fresh challenge. This happened in all speedway teams, so looking back to see who had rode for Mildenhall the most times from the very first meeting Robert Henry topped the list with a staggering 434 appearances. The next four riders on this list who all raced over 200 times for the Fen Tigers were all from the early days - Mick Bates, Ray Bales, Melvyn Taylor and Richard Knight.

For the first Academy League encounter, Mildenhall were due to entertain Stoke Potters with a change at number seven where Darren Andrews was riding. Once again, the home team felt the bitter taste of a defeat when Stoke won 57-39, although this turned out to be a challenge match instead as Stoke (calling themselves the Potteries Select) were still awaiting the official go-ahead to ride as Stoke. It looked to be a long hard season for the Tigers stretching before them. Andy Giddings and Tony Kingsbury were the only two heat winners for the Tigers and team manager said he would be leaving no stone unturned to strengthen the team after a below average performance. A Four-Team Tournament filled in another week with the Fen Tigers up against quartets from Sittingbourne, Cleveland and Exeter. The Crusaders from Kent ending winners with the Tigers close on two points away. The Fen/Tweed Trophy ended as expected in Berwick's hands as they chalked up a big victory over Mildenhall in the Border country; Gary Sweet top scoring with fourteen and young second half rider Richard Watts made up the team at the last minute and showed determination although he did not score any points.

Mildenhall broke their duck when Linlithgow Lightening came to visit, the Tigers winning 66-30, although the Scottish team borrowed Richard Watts when one of their riders failed to turn up at West Row. After winning the Opportunity Race Roger Horspool, who was signed on loan, was quickly fed into the main team and responded with a score of paid twelve-point maximum from the number seven spot. He had just come back into the sport after taking a three year break

Old favourites and near rivals Sittingbourne were next up and had come back into the league naming their track the Marshbank Stadium. This was the first leg of the knockout cup and the Fen Tigers had just returned to base after two away meetings at Exeter and Cradley Heath, the latter which was a challenge match. It produced a spirited win at Exeter on their much bigger track 56-40, and a loss 42-36 in the midlands, which went to a last heat decider, and where Chris Storey came into the Tigers side scoring four points from his three rides. Richard Watts also had his second outing for Mildenhall at Cradley. The Tigers registered a big win over Sittingbourne to take to the second leg in Kent. Their number one Kevin Teager notched up the highest score of the meeting with seventeen points, a job well done by the Suffolk born rider who was approaching his thirty-seventh birthday.

Mildenhall made it three wins out of three in the league with a home victory against Cleveland Bays 56-40 as they looked a solid side with heat leaders Simon Wolstenholme and Gary Sweet in double figures together with newcomer Roger Horspool chalking up a paid maximum once again from the number seven position. More young riders were treading the road to the West Row Stadium for rides and names such as Simon Brown, Freddie Stephenson, Darren Brinkhoff and Gavin Pell were seen in the second halfs. There was also the early appearances of a Nathan Morton plus a fleeting glimpse of a certain Tony Childs, a blast from the past? At the Tigers trip to Sittingbourne, Storey and Watts took rides in the second half to widen their away tracks experience. It was also at Sittingbourne that the full force of the Mildenhall away support

-14-

was really felt with many supporters making the short journey to cheer on their favourites.

A vacant Sunday was taken up with a match versus a North-East Select (a mixture of Berwick and Cleveland riders, who were the opposition for the Michael Lee Trophy. The former World Champion had made available this trophy for competition and was on hand to present it to the winning team. This particular trophy ended up on the Fen Tigers shelf by reason of their 61-32 win on the afternoon. For this meeting Roger Horspool had built up an average of over eleven and was in the team proper.

A weekend away of exhausting proportions was the Mildenhall lot when they faced Berwick on Saturday evening and then on to Cleveland for a Sunday match. Both encounters were lost but could well have been closer and perhaps one a win. Berwick Bandits were proving the strongest team in the Academy League, but the following meeting saw some controversial decisions going the opposite way from the Tigers, which also saw one of the lowest attendances at a Mildenhall match away from home. Luck was with the Fen Tigers when on the journey to their digs for the night in Berwick, Dean Garrod's van caught fire from a battery they were carrying. However, Malcolm Vasey who was just in front stopped quickly and helped quench the flames and save the bikes. Dingle Brown and the Sweet family also arrived on the scene to help with what could well have been a disaster. But that is the way the Mildenhall teamwork happens.

The weather decided to plague Mildenhall in their next home meeting when Buxton were the visiting team, where in spite of the wet conditions and rainfall the meeting started. The circumstances were not good, it was shown in the heat time's right from the start, and times of over one minute were laid out. It was after six slow heats that the referee Mr Graham Brodie called it off. There was a thought that re-grading the track and adding more dirt was the solution but this notion was discarded and everyone departed for home a little earlier than expected. Many of them did not have the chance of watching a slightly unusual second half, which had sidecar speedway racing for the first time ever. Although the statutory six heats had been completed for no refund the

Mildenhall promoters decided to accept the re-admission tickets for the next meeting at West Row for the British Speedway Academy League Grand Prix; the supporters who had stood waiting in the rain the previous week entering free. The public were always well catered for by the Tigers promotion and the programmes featured quizzes, crosswords and even a word-search on some occasions.

The League table up to the end of July showed Berwick Bandits sitting on top by reason of winning all their five matches, Buxton Hit-Men in second spot and the Fen Tigers third, winning three and losing two of their meetings. The Devon Devils occupied bottom place having lost six of their seven matches, but it was not yet halfway. All the Academy League teams provided a pair of riders for the Grand Prix meeting, Mildenhall being represented by Roger Horspool and Dean Garrod who took the place of Gary Sweet who had badly damaged his knee at Stoke the night before, and which ended his season early. The Sittingbourne pairing of Teager and Mason were the winners.

Back at Mildenhall base there were changes in the promotion when illness saw Derek Hewitt hand over the full reigns to Dingle Brown. Nevertheless, one bright light in what was fast becoming a bad dream with injuries; Horspool was proving a fine signing and led the scoreline at many meetings. At this part of the season, Garrod and Giddings were both on the injured list together with Sweet. Setting out for the Stoke KO Cup meeting Mildenhall only had three riders available (Sweet, Garrod and Horspool) Tony Kingsbury then turned up complete with a new engine and Jonathan Swales and Brian Turner were hastily signed from the now defunct Cleveland Bays. Storey completed a patched-up team. After this match Turner went out on loan to Linlithgow.

Bottom team Exeter, under the guise of the Devon Demons came to West Row and their pairing of captain Graeme Gordon and Scott Peglar got thirty of their total of thirty-nine between them as they saw the points go to Mildenhall whose top scorer was newcomer Jonathan Swales. Two Reserves (Storey and Kingsbury) were promoted into the Tigers line-up and done a wonderful job.

Having a multi-purpose stadium had its drawbacks when the home
-16-

meeting against Sittingbourne on 27 August caused problems. Despite doing all they could to overcome the issue with the Greyhound Racing, which had made the stadium out of limits for one week, the promoters of the Fen Tigers, together with Mr Terry Waters, there were no speedway on that day, and the match was slotted in later in the summer.

The Berwick Bandits came to West Row as an unbeaten team in September, and with the Fen Tigers unbeaten in the league at home, something had to give in this meeting. Unfortunately, the British summer weather intervened and the meeting was abandoned after nine very wet heats, and with the visitors leading 36-18 and just one Fen Tiger winning a race. Of the various falls Jonathan Swales injured hand put him out of the next few weeks, not to mention the £300 worth of damage to his bike. The Veteran Speedway Riders Association were the Mildenhall guests at this meeting with wives and families, and they all were delighted with the roast lunch provided for them in the restaurant. Four times World Speedway Champions Barry Briggs was also at West Row and said how much he enjoyed the racing as it was in the damp conditions.

The next two meetings were cancelled as the weather stayed stormy and wet for a long period and the fixture list for the remainder of the season bore no resemblance to the original. The fixtures were completed eventually with home defeats inflicted on the Tigers by Sittingbourne and Stoke (KO Cup) but ended on a higher note with a win over Buxton in the re-arranged fixture rained-off in July. Although not fans of 'rider-replacement', the Mildenhall team had to ride this way for the final matches. Altogether, it was a fragmented season with Gary Sweet, Simon Wolstenholme, Jonathan Swales, Peter Boast, Dean Garrod, Andy Giddings, Colin Cage and Clive Clark all having spells on the injured list. Mildenhall were lucky however to secure the services of Geoff Powel towards the end of the season, who had spent most of his career so far in the Northern reaches of the British Isles. Nick-named 'Leggy' he put in some very good performances and the Tigers were seriously hoping he makes the journey from Cumbria next season to West Row. The only ever-present rider was Tony Kingsbury as Mildenhall ended up in fifth place out of seven teams.

Feelers were put out for a large screen to have a 'Video Night' during the winters break, together with the Grand Presentation Evening at the stadium and for the first time a 'Christmas Party in December. As well as the riders at these 'Do's' the track staff were to be guests as a thank you for their great work in what was a very up and down season. The track itself was now settling down now that Robert 'Huggy' Huggins was back in the fold; having been in charge several years previous and was also a great friend to everyone. Having Stock Cars on Saturday evenings before a Sunday Speedway meeting was not the ideal factor and all staff worked at it to stage the speedway on a fair track.

Mildenhall with its acknowledgement towards bringing young and first-time riders through the ranks, was selected as the venue during October for the Southern Track Riders 'Open Championship'. This took place on the first of the month after the meeting Mildenhall versus Stoke. All those taking part were amateur riders who had been at training schools at various tracks and on show were some of the Mildenhall school including Freddie Stephenson, Simon Brown, Mark Czyx and Gavin Pell. Crowned the champion was Steve Targett who chalked up four wins and a second place, with the home track's Gavin Pell as runner-up. Altogether a well worthwhile exercise for all concerned.

The final meeting of 1995 was a Best Pairs Championship with all the Mildenhall riders and some second-half riders took part with some special guests including Mike Hampson (Buxton). An interesting pair was Simon Wolstenholme with his namesake David while the top pair scoring twenty-two points each saw a run-off for first place between Steve Knott and Gavin Pell take the honours from Dean Garrod and his partner Tony Kingsbury.

****

1996

Yet another change of name for the Academy League as it took the title of the Conference League. This was the season when the league champions were decided on percentages and not points, as the thirteen teams could run as many meetings as they could fit in. This was thought to benefit those teams with very limited dates to use their home track; teams were also made up of six riders plus one meeting reserve. Nearly every club ran a different number of meetings as the league table looked

-18-

rather a mess for most of the year, only becoming slightly better when the season had ended. The speedway bosses in their wisdom had decided to run the Conference League in this way but it was not satisfactory in many different ways and was quickly forgotten the next year. They had not taken into consideration the quote that "if it is not causing any problems don't change it!"

On the broader sphere of the speedway world, the sport was re-emerging in London with the forming of the London Lions while Cradley Heath had moved into Stoke as the search went on for a new track of their own. Edinburgh went to race at Glasgow and called themselves the Scottish Monarchs, and this was a move in the right direction to keep speedway alive in both Edinburgh and Glasgow.

The one disappointment when the riders for the new season were announced was that Roger Horspool was not amongst them; he had decided to retire from riding. Gary Sweet was on the list but was not expected to return from his long term injury until after the season got underway. He was due to have another operation on his troublesome knee injury. One happy event was the marriage in March of Gary and Michelle. Geoff Powell was considered the top man when he elected to ride for the Fen Tigers to everyone's delight. Dingle Brown also had a new position that of chairman of the club and he announced "I must thank our landlord Mr Terry Waters for all the work carried out during the winter months. The stadium is an excellent facility and we must strive to match it by producing entertainment of the highest quality in a happy environment with a common purpose. This is to make the Fen Tigers one of the most respected and feared Speedway teams in the land."

On top of the injuries to man and machine the previous year, sponsorship was on every riders mind, and a list of how the expenses mount up for each meeting. Taking in things such as travelling, racing oil, lubricants, together with items like tyres, clutch, chain, goggles and general wear and tear it was noted that it cost a rider around £90 each meeting. One of the most popular ways for the supporters to help out was the scheme to sponsor one pound for each point a rider gets, and many of the Mildenhall fans took this up. Yet another innovation was

(1) FEN TIGERS LINE-UP 1992

(2) MIKAEL TUERNBERG

(3) JESPER OLSEN

**(4 top) DINGLE BROWN, DEAN GARROD, GEOFF POWELL
(4 bottom) WAYNE BROADHURST**

the publication in the programme of a map showing where the stadium is in relation to surrounding towns. So there would be no excuse about not knowing where the meeting was.

The new season opened on Sunday 14 April with the British Under 21 Championship (semi-final). Some of the best of the youngsters coming through were in this competition and at West Row were future stars including Lee Richardson (Reading) Stuart Swales (Cradley) and Blair Scott (Linlithgow). Coming out on top was Swales and the top four went through to the final. It was a meeting that saw all the heats run with no fallen riders and only one exclusion for touching the tapes; this was not seen at many meetings at that time. While things were going perfectly on track there were problems elsewhere when the PA system failed completely together with a malfunction of the radio microphone, but the presenter and others managed to get through the meeting with a great deal of running about to keep pace with the action.

The last weekend in April saw the Essex Open Championship at Arena Essex, with Mildenhall's Dean Garrod finishing in a creditable joint third place and Jonathan Swales also reaching double figures. Young Simon Brown was the meetings reserve and managed to gain one point from his ride.

Before starting on the league fixtures Mildenhall faced Arena Essex Hammers home and away in what was termed the Spring Gold Cup. The away leg went the Tigers way by 52-26, the only downside of this was Geoff Powell having the use of Peter Boast's second bike as he managed to blow his engine on the 'Press Day' at West Row. A second blown engine came the way of Tony Kingsbury but with no encouragement, the fans on the terraces made a collection for Tony as a large bill was in the offing. At home, Mildenhall won once more 48-30 to claim the first piece of silverware of the season. Peter Boast chalking up a fifteen point paid maximum, and wearing the captain's hat as well. One innovation was the filming of each Mildenhall meeting and supporters being able to buy copies to sit and view through the dark winter months. Berwick Bandits were then invited to test just how good were the Fen Tigers, this was the first leg of the Fen/Tweed Trophy, but in fact, the second leg was never raced in 1996. This meeting spelt out just how far the Tigers have to improve to match their visitors who were the league champions last year; and champions of the Third Division in 1994; Berwick winning 41-35. There was however, some excellent racing as Mildenhall clawed back from nine points behind to run the Bandits quite close. A new name entered the Tigers team as Charlie Whitwam was the number seven and had one ride but not scoring. He must have impressed as the next home meeting against the new Reading Ravens (45-32) he was in the main team registering two fruitless rides combined with two falls, but the enthusiasm and determination led to him being given more meetings as the season progressed. He was not the only one to fall off against Reading as Powell reeled off four straight wins only to suffer a fall in the last race of the day.

News of a former Mildenhall rider from the early nineties came when Savalas Clouting won the British Under 21 Championship held at Swindon. He had joined the Fen Tigers in the fateful 1992 season hoping for a team place but did not actually ride. He was now at Ipswich and he was just in front of his team-mate Scott Nicholls who was runner-up. Two real heroes from yesteryear were seen at West Row, Tiger Beach and Trevor Barnwell; of course, you remember them, don't you? Another well-known name from the Speedway world sadly passed away; Howdy Byford had a long career stretching over twenty years. An up and coming rider of the future was seen in the second half at West Row when Mark Thompson was trying his luck; He had already made his debut with Sittingbourne versus Exeter but was to make a significant part of Mildenhall's future later on.

The Fen Tigers travelled to the Derbyshire Dales to be the first team to race on the Buxton Hitman's brand new track. This had been built next to the stock-car arena where they had shared the condition with the cars, but now they were quite independent to this. Geoff Powell was forced to withdraw after three heats when an old injury flared up once more. Boast and Garrod reached double figures but the rest of the team could not get to terms with the somewhat bumpy racing strip.

Back in East Anglia, the operation at Kings Lynn was forced to close down for 1996 but hopes were high of being active for the next year. This meant quite a few Lynn supporters were making their way to the

West Row stadium for their weekly fix of speedway and one wrote to the Mildenhall management. "Now reduced to floating fans may I say how much we and our friends enjoyed our visit to see the match against Berwick. We found the facilities good, the stadium tidy, and best of all we enjoyed the racing. The people were friendly and we met some more Kings Lynn fans as well. A.Moy (Aylsham.) Another letter thought "I heard that Mildenhall are ambitious and they would like to advance to a higher level; forget it, it's the clubs in the Premier League that need to show ambition, by trying to reach the high standard set by this lovely little Suffolk venue."

The Tigers switched to a Saturday night meeting when Linlithgow Lightning came to visit, and looked to improve on their home meeting with the Tigers at their picturesque Heathersfield Stadium in the hills, where they were the victors 42-34. The Mildenhall bikes in particular suffered damage, no more so than Jonathan Swales in a spectacular coming together, also leaving him with aggravating an old wrist injury. In the return meeting, the Lightening put it across Mildenhall once again (44-34) as the homesters only managed to provide four heat winners. Linlithgow also borrowed young Mark Thompson and gave him one ride, from which he had a pointless outing. Mark had already made his debut in the third tier with an outing for Sittingbourne against Exeter in May.

To bolster up the Tigers side Steve Knott was brought in on loan for the season having been on the books of Cradley Heath and Stoke, and having had a few rides for Mildenhall in 1994. He took the place of Charlie Whitwam who has not let the side down but had tried too hard on occasions, even riding carrying an injury, but he had collected a broken collarbone in the win at Eastbourne. He was certain to return at some later stage as he was one earmarked for the future. The victory in Sussex was the first away points of the season and at a track, which has not been kind to Mildenhall over the years. Geoff Powell was again on top form with a fifteen-point maximum once again. The following day the Tigers made the long journey and across the water to the Isle of Wight to face the Wight Wizards. This was the first time on the Island and the Wizards won by ten points; the high being the great number of Mildenhall supporters who made the trip to cheer on their team. Further honours befell Malcolm Vasey the West Row announcer when he was asked to do the same job for the Tigers match there; Eastbourne was another to seek Malcolm's services and two extra names on his CV. The Tigers made up for this with a return to winning ways at home to Buxton 46-32.

Forsaking the league programme the Fen Tigers had the semi-final of the League Knockout Cup to contend with, Arena Essex Hammers being their opponents for the home leg first. Old hand Peter Thorogood was their man in charge and they had improved since the early season encounter with Mildenhall, and it was rather a surprise that they seemed to surrender easily as Mildenhall set up a extremely good points lead to take to the second leg, the score being 56-22. The Tigers then were brought back down to earth in a big way when their next visitors, the Devon Demons, stole the points when they were the winners by two points (40-38). Before the racing could get underway, poor Steve Knott suffered a blown engine and although borrowing Simon Brown's bike for his first ride he was not happy with this and actually walked out of the stadium. Reserve Peter Grimwood took his other three rides without scoring. The Demons also borrowed Malcolm Hogg for number seven but he did not get a ride. The Tigers made up for this by supplying all four riders for the Second Half final. Some top league teams were also looking at the lower league riders and Mildenhall's Peter Boast rode as a guest at Hull.

Continuing the diet of weekly home meetings for a period the league leaders were up next. The Isle of Wight Wizards were going strongly under the guidance of team manager George Major the ex Birmingham rider of distinction. The Fen Tigers however proceeded to cast a spell over the Wizards and were victors by a margin of ten points (44-34). New Tigers signing Jason Gage broke down on the way to West Row and having had to leave his bike behind he arrived at the stadium and borrowed Dean Garrod's spare bike and notched up a useful score of nine points. It must be said the Wizards were at a disadvantage when three of their top riders were injured, on the Friday night riding at Arena Essex and Eastbourne on Saturday evening. The Tigers management also were on hand to help them find replacements. Former Mildenhall Simon Wolstenholme was signed on as an emergency and they included

-23-

the young American Buck Blair who took six rides and scored 13+2 points. He was an instant hit with the crowd and was looked upon as having a very successful career in front of him. Blair had been hanging around at Mildenhall for nearly two years while the BSPA advised the Fen Tigers not to let him ride for the them in the Conference League, although there was noting really by law to stop him doing just that. This was proved when the Isle of Wight Wizards did not have any comebacks in borrowing him at West Row. However, in the end the youngster from the United States was tired of waiting around and retired back to his homeland.

Mildenhall carried on their home spell as Sittingbourne Crusaders were beaten 52-25 with all the team scoring well, but the top points-man on the night was the visiting captain and number one David Mason who chalked up seventeen points from his six outings, only being pushed into second place in the first heat by the Fen Tigers Geoff Powell. Also in the Sittingbourne side was Mark Czyz who had been having many second half outings at West Row.

The Mildenhall supporters were always up for anything new and the Rye House Supporters Club challenged them to a darts match after the meeting on 7 July in the clubroom. This effort provided a great success as Mildenhall were the top darts sharpshooters by 42-36, and little trophy's were even presented to the winners. A return match is already in the pipeline. As with many rivals in the speedway world, much is made of the two promotions going for each other's throat but underneath it all they were nearly always the best of friends. This was true of Mildenhall and Rye House fans and riders, as was seen on more than one occasion. After the Saturday night meeting, a Disco was planned after the racing finished and after a further Sunday meeting the clubroom was the venue for a Quiz night.

The way in which Mildenhall looks after the younger rider and those just making their way in the speedway world was non-more brought to the fore with a letter from one such youngster, and which was re-printed in the programme. "On behalf of myself (Glen Bocking) and all the second half riders, we would like to say many thanks to all the management, track staff, St Johns and everybody else involved in

-24-

running the Mildenhall Speedway. These people create such a friendly atmosphere and without their help and support, we would not be able to ride. The facilities are all first class."

Completing the second leg of the semi-final of the Knock-out Cup at Sittingbourne, Simon Brown came into the Tigers side in place of Jason Gage who took time off as his wife had been involved in a car crash, fortunately not too serious. Mark Thompson was at number seven for his first competitive meeting and scoring one point as Mildenhall came through to the final quite easily. On 11 August the Berwick Bandits made their second visit of the season to West Row and the home team had their revenge for the earlier defeat by winning this one 41-37 as Powell chalked up another fifteen point maximum. It was a shame that the weather kept the crowd down for this encounter.

The following meeting gave the fans a great deal for their money when the Tigers took on the Arena Essex Hammers, which was followed by a full thirteen-heat match between the two Reserve teams of the clubs. The Mildenhall seven were Simon Brown (captain), David Nix, Malcolm Hogg, Charlie Whitwam, Darren Smith, Mark Thompson and Peter Grimwood, and they backed up the good first team's performance with a win. The first team won their contest 59-19 as the Hammers failed to provide a heat winner, their top scorer being Gavin Pell on six points. When Mildenhalll won 52-26 over the Sheffield (Owlerton) Prowlers, the Fen Tigers number one Geoff registered his third fifteen point full maximum in succession at West Row. The visitors had to borrow Charlie Whitwam who scored them two points from his single ride. While Charlie had often caused sparks on the track, a fire started in the electric cables in the greyhound kennels part of the stadium, which knocked out the Tannoy system. The fire was soon put out and announcer Malcolm Vasey had to resort to running around the track to try to get his messages over to the supporters.

The Berwick team then turned up again at Mildenhall, this was allowed by the league rules for this season when this could happen if everyone agreed, and this time the Border side took both points after a narrow victory 41-37. The Conference League Riders Championship meeting was at Long Eaton and the Mildenhall representative was Dean

Garrod and was not disgraced with his haul of six points. The champion was Mike Hampson of Buxton, which were the next ones to come to West Row for a League meeting. Whitwam was back in the Tigers line-up and young David Nix had two rides for the visitors from the Reserve berth. The newly crowned Riders champion Mike Hampson reeled off five straight heat wins but was involved in a last heat crash that resulted in a dislocated shoulder and a damaged wrist. His partner was also had a stretcher ride with a broke ankle.

Friday the thirteenth proved very unlucky for the Fen Tigers at Arena Essex when they went under by twelve points (45-33). Tony Kingsbury was out injured and after rearing at the gate Jason Gage, after completing the re-run, he had to withdraw from the meeting. The big invitation meeting of the year was the Bernie Klatt Memorial Trophy meeting and the list of riders included those from nearly all the Conference League teams, but unfortunately, eight heats only were completed before the rain struck once again and the meeting had to be abandoned.

The Conference League KO Cup Final saw Mildenhall up against Linlithgow, with the Scottish team already the league champions. On their home track, Linlithgow Lightning were practically unbeatable and although Mildenhall tried to keep the score respectable, they lost the first leg 49-29. It looked as if the Lightning had only to turn up in the return leg to grab the cup.

The Final was part of the Fen Tigers yearly trek to the North and Scotland to take on Berwick and Linlithgow. The Berwick meeting was a series of engine problems for the riders and Whitwam had another argument with the safety fence, spending a night in hospital before limping on crutches, he travelled with the team to support the lads in the Linlithgow encounter. The Mildenhall supporters enjoyed the two-day trip as well travelling by luxury coach and staying in a specially reserved hotel, and all this for just £48 each. They were certainly the most travelled fans in the Conference League. The second leg of the Cup Final at West Row was a closer match and ended as a draw at thirty-nine points each and the cup went to Scotland. The Tigers provided the top scorer in Jonathan Swales who put together thirteen hard-earned points. Darren Smith made a first appearance at number seven for the Tigers; one ride for one point; this was his only time in the team and he had to wait another eight years before appearing in the Tigers colours again. *This meeting drew a bumper crowd including a coach load from Scotland.*

The Bernie Klatt Memorial Trophy meeting was eventually re-run on 27 October with most of the original riders returning for the second time of asking, and the season was wound down with a Best Pairs Competition. Geoff Powell finished the season with an average of 9-29 and Dean Garrod was an ever-present in the team as well as the Mildenhall representative in the Conference Riders Championship, taking the place of Powell who was deemed ineligible (too old) to take part as the League was more for youngsters learning the art of speedway; he was thirty-four. One of the best things to come from this season was that the attendances had picked up at West Row where the Fen Tigers were always value for money. Mildenhall rode nineteen meetings to end in mid-table with twenty-two points

The occasions' were not finished however as the Presentation Evening took place on 2 November at the Stadium Club House with a three-course buffet followed by a Disco until late in the evening, and all the riders attended this one to everyone's enjoyment. Some even ventured to say it was the best night ever, or at least up to that period. The next month a Christmas Party and Disco was arranged for a Saturday night the 14 December.

****

1997

The new season brought with it a profound problem to solve. The Elite League came into being as the top tier, the Premier League was more or less Division Two and the Conference League was subject to yet another conversion of name; this time the British Amateur League. This saw several of the ex Conference teams opt to join the new Premier League, which meant the Amateur League was seen as a training league for the Elite Clubs as well as some Premier teams. Supporters of the Fen Tigers were used to more than training matches, but Promoter Dingle Brown was concerned that the average gate at West Row might not be enough to keep the club going, and no one wanted it to go bankrupt. If this happened, the enforced closure would probably have meant that speedway would disappear forever for the Fen Tigers.

The British Amateur League was chosen for Mildenhall but they still signed the riders they thought would uphold the tradition of the Fen Tigers and not be dictated to by the Godfather's of British Speedway. (Old!) Geoff Powell was retained to lead the Mildenhall seven once again. Powell was a vastly experienced rider, having spent well over a decade at Glasgow Tigers before switching to the Fen Tigers in 1996. Youngster Gavin Pell had only one season in the sport before gaining a place in the Tigers side, having been an accomplished rider for Arena Essex the year before. Gary Sweet was associated with the Wimbledon juniors before moving to Mildenhall, and was joined in the Tigers set-up by his younger brother Chris Sweet. Twenty-year-old Dean Garrod came through the Mildenhall training sessions, progressing to second half rides and was in the team at sixteen years of age. Nathan Morton was expected to do well as a heat-leader after impressing at Conference level at Arena Essex the year before. The supporters favourite and always exciting rider was also back at West Row; Charlie Whitwam. Signing in late June was Dean Chapman ex-captain of the Sittingbourne Crusaders in 1996.

Competing in the new league were Ryde (IOW), M4 Sprockets (Swindon & Reading), Belle Vue, Buxton, Berwick, Welsh Warriers (Newport & Exeter), Lathallan, St Austell, Oxford, Mildenhall, Peterborough and Anglian Angels (Kings Lynn & Ipswich). Quite an impressive motley crew. For this season, the sponsorship meant that it was Mildenhall 'Profire Protection' Fen Tigers

Monday 7 April was the opening fixture in the newly named league as Mildenhall visited the Wight Wizards (Ryde) on the Isle of Wight for a tough match. This was especially so for new captain Powell who crashed in the first heat and then suffering another horrific pile-up in heat eight when the Ryde pair of Eldridge and Crook together with Powell saw men and machinery fly in all directions. The Tigers number one picked himself up and claimed second place in the re-run on Dean Garrod's bike. New man Nathan Morton top scored with nine points in a match that also saw Garry Sweet back in the saddle after a long and

-28-

serious injury. When the dust settled the final score was 48-30 to the Wizards.

The return fixture was the following Sunday when the Wizards again waved their wands and took the points once again with a 40-38 scoreline in their favour. Powell led from the front for the Tigers but his seventeen-point haul was not quite enough, as Garry Sweet and Morton were only other two to ride with any conviction at West Row. Geoff Powell had become a firm favourite at Mildenhall after most of his early riding had been in Scotland and the North of England (Glasgow, Newcastle & Linlithgow) his home being in Cumbria.

A visit to Peterborough resulted in three matches played and all three lost by the Fen Tigers, although the third match saw no Geoff Powell, 'Leggy' to his friends, as he had work commitments, and once again problems were experienced with the machinery, including a blown engine for Nathan Morton Whitwam came into the side and scored a healthy six points, but experiencing a fall in his last race. The visit of the Anglian Angels to West Row then got the |Tigers up and winning 53-25. At last. The win was somewhat marred by the crash by Mark Thompson, now in the Anglian side, when he suffered a multi-leg fracture, and in the last heat too.

The Tigers Northern tour this year was a welcome success with superb performances at Berwick (a draw) and Lathallan (a win in atrocious conditions), giving the travelling supporters something to really cheer about. The most satisfying was the point at Berwick, the first point anyone has taken from them at home since they re-formed in 1994. Another combination side was the next home meeting; the Long Eaton/Wolverhampton side had joined the league in the last minute, and managed by ex Premier Rider Martin Dixon. Captain Powell and Dean Garrod each contributed a maximum to help Mildenhall to a 47-31 victory.

Away at Newport versus the Welsh Warriers, at their new stadium at Queensway Meadows, the home side won 39-37 with Geoff Powell suffering problems in two of his heats, blowing his engine at the tapes and shedding a chain, coupled with two victories and a third place. Dean

Garrod was the top Tiger scoring fifteen points, and Gary Sweet managed nine, but the remaining riders only scored six points between them. All on a very wet track. A switch was made to a Saturday evening versus Peterborough Thundercats who tracked the young impressive David Howe and former Mildenhall captain Gavin Hedge together with West Row second-haft racer Freddie Stevenson. Drawn match a thirty-nine each. It seemed at times that every team that came to West Row contained at least one rider who had assisted the Tigers in previous years, and Lathallan Lightning paraded Jonathan Swales who had two seasons at West Row. The Scottish outfit were sent home pointless as Mildenhall recorded another home win as they began to steadily pick up points.

A surprise came after this match when Peterborough Thundercats arrived in the pits and proceeded to ride another match after the Tigers had finished, against the same Lathallan team. Their clash the night before had been rained off at the East of England Showground and to save the team from Scotland making another long trip to the East of England, Peterborough managers had asked Dingle Brown if they could stage their match at West Row. Of course after asking the track staff and others involved in running a meeting this was agreed. Mildenhall were pleased to be able to help another club out of a hole, even if it was rivals Peterborough. Dingle had first been approached about this arrangement when on his way to Belle Vue when the Mildenhall match there was called off due to the pouring rain.

Journeying to Oxford Cubs the next day (Sunday), Mildenhall came away with the win by 41-37 in a close encounter, which saw over half the heats shared at three points each. Together with Powell, Garrod, Pell, Chapman, Gary Sweet and Chris Sweet, Jamie Barton made up the team. It was Gary Sweet's night as he top scored with 10 points closely followed by Powell on 9. Newcomer Barton scored a well-merited seven points when coming into the team for Morton who was resting a knee injury for a while. Oxford supplied eight heat winners and Mildenhall only five but the visitors filled most of the other scoring places to give them a moral-boosting victory.

As of last year, the Supporters Club was running coach trips to most of the away meetings and the first to fill up quickly was the trip to the

Derbyshire hills for the Buxton match. Leaving Bishops Stortford at eight in the morning it called at Mildenhall Stadium around nine, and on to the Dales. Unfortunately the rain decided to make an appearance and the Hitmen managed in the conditions better that the Fen Tigers although the score-line of 44-33 does not do the Tigers any favours as it was only in the last three heats that the home team got well in front. Charlie Whitwam was feeling his back injury and was missing a few matches and at Buxton young David Osborne rode in his first ever meeting; he was the son of former Scunthorpe promoter several years before. The trip to Cornwall and St Austell was another, which attracted a full coach as well, to see the extraordinarily unusual St Austell stadium, built in a quarry in the West of the country. This coach trip was turned into a two-day break with bed-and-breakfast on the Tuesday night. However, this trip did not materialise as the match was postponed because of rain.

As well as looking after the young riders of the future and running training sessions at the track, the Mildenhall Supporters Club did the same for the young children who came each week to cheer on their hero's. Calling these supporters the Fen Tiger Cubs they were all entered in a free draw each home meeting. The winner each time had the opportunity to be invited to the pits area and have their photograph taken with their favourite rider. Quite an incentive for the children and to keep them interested enough to keep coming to West Row, and of course bringing along mum and dad. For the older fans, Quiz Nights were the order of the day after the meeting finished with more dart matches on the bill as well.

Mildenhall team manager Dingle Brown even got himself on the television screen around this time when the 'Eastenders' programme went for a story-line which involved a speedway meeting. He had to go along to 'shoot' this episode, which also saw Nathan Morton and a Tigers new signing Jamie Barton also being involved as well. Dingle managed to get himself a nice bright red blazer so that he could be picked out easily in the part of the programme that was actually filmed at the Arena Essex track.

Into July and Mildenhall had for their opponents at West Row the

-31-

combined team of Newport and Exeter, and a chance for the Fen Tigers to gain revenge for their earlier loss down in Wales. This they did 44-33. Belle Vue Colts then suffered the same fate 41-37. Ever ready to help other clubs Mildenhall agreed to start this home meeting earlier in the day to allow the Belle Vue supporters to take in their senior teams match versus Peterborough in the same evening. Recognition came the way of Dean Garrod when he was asked to ride as a guest for the Newport side, and weighed in with three plus one bonus points for the South Wales team. There were several open week-ends in the fixtures as one rule from the BSPA management saw just twelve meetings at home for all clubs and no other meetings at all.

Lying halfway down the League table the Fen Tigers went out and acquired Anthony Barlow from Berwick to give them an extra boost and strengthen the lower order. He had an average of over nine at the time, and he made his debut against Oxford Cubs at West Row where he contributed a paid seven score in the Tigers win, despite having some bike problems. He had arrived at West Row from his home in Southport with the rear tyre on his bike having suddenly exploded in the back of his van as he was travelling along, Mildenhall's Powell lending him a spare one for the meeting. Another rider who had been missing for a time was the loan rider from Arena Essex, Nathan Morton who had recovered from a bad injury to his foot. Promoter Dingle Brown thought this was one of the strongest line-ups he had put out for quite a time, and looked confident after the Tigers had already won at Oxford. Former Tigers skipper Simon Wolstenholme led Oxford and together with Lee Driver were the only steady scorers for the visitors.

This victory was the beginning of a good run of form and for a while, the top of the league was thought to be within their grasp, but it was not to be and they ended the season in fifth place. Unfortunately, this meeting also saw the one and only one for Anthony Barlow as he had a falling out with the Mildenhall promotion and moved on quickly to Oxford the next week. He had decided not to travel down to Suffolk as he thought Newcastle wanted him in the Premier League, a decision that did not please the Mildenhall promoters, and it was announced to the supporters that he was not in the Fen Tigers plans for the future. At this latter meeting young 11=-year-old Karl Mason as he journeyed round the speedway tracks and riding round to raise money for the BBC Children-in-Need appeal, and getting fans to sponsor him. Karl was the Stoke and Buxton mascot and he made just over one hundred and fifteen pounds for his appeal at West Row.

Mildenhall 30 Berwick Bandits 47 was a disappointing score-line and it seemed that the Bandits were proving a bogy team for the Fen Tigers. After heat ten the home team were just four points behind and looked to be capable of overhauling the visitors, but then a 5-0 followed by two 5-1's made the defeat look more convincing than it really was. Reserve Dean Chapman moved up into the main team in place of Barlow and Chris Sweet had another outing at number seven. Then the away meeting at Reading went to a last heat decider and Mildenhall lost by two points (40-38).

The next match against St Austell Gulls saw the first appearance in Mildenhall colours of Gavin Hedge who had been riding for Peterborough, Skegness and Isle of Wight. He was thought to have some good potential and would prove a good signing, and more reliable than former new signing Barlow would. The win over St Austell was a team performance with everyone scoring well, and the Fen Tigers followed this up with a 46-26 victory away at Belle Vue in what was described as a very clinical performance, with the Chairman venturing that he had felt very proud watching the team in that win. This match was also one in which Jamie Barton won his first heat for the Tigers.

Dean Garrod was the Mildenhall representative in the League Riders Championship at Long Eaton where the Supporters Club ran a coach to give him their support; he finished with seven points but picked up the award from the sponsors for the 'best non-winner'. Another winner was our own Malcolm Vasey who took time out to get married to Desiree during August, Dingle Foot acting as best man.

In the push to finish as high as possible in the league Mildenhall then swept the M4 Raven Sprockets (Reading/Swindon) aside 52-26, captain Geoff Powell being in exceptional form with five wins in his five races, Garry Sweet scored five second places; three behind a team-mate, while newcomer Hedge reached double figures. Even in the second half final, it read 1st=Powell, 2nd=Hedge and 3rd=Sweet. It was generally thought in many quarters that had the Tigers tracked the team now performing so well from the beginning the League Championship could have been well within their grasp. The final meeting of the year was on a Saturday evening versus the might of Buxton Hitmen on the last week-end in September. They had in their side the Riders Champion in Jon Armstrong. A final all-round team effort ended the season with a 40-38 win. Over all it had been a frustrating year and fans, riders and management alike felt they could have topped the league if the several close matches had gone the Tigers way instead of against them; fifth place was the Mildenhall lot at the finish

The End of Season Presentation Evening this year was a Dinner and Dance with a live band, and was a great success with all tickets sold for the evening where supporters and riders alike celebrated a very good season. All the riders were given an engraved plaque for their services and Geoff Powell also having a trophy presented to him by his number one fan Sean. James Barton was the recipient of the Cook Memorial Shield presented by Vi Cook in memory of her husband who was a great follower of speedway. The team looked as if they would be fighting for honours the next year. As well as this special evening, there was also the annual Christmas party and buffet

****

1998

Frustration had been the name of the game throughout the previous season, and there was hope for a change in the organisation and system in the league set-up; Mildenhall got their wish. At the beginning of 1998 there was a new name for the league and sponsored by Dunlop it became the Dunlop Conference League. There was also a new format of fifteen heats, the last heat being for nominated riders. Each rider must have a minimum of two rides, and a maximum of six teams were allowed to use one Premier League rider, who had an average below four points. Once he went above this, he was not allowed to ride in the lower league.It was hard to keep track of all the happenings around this novel rule, and by the end of the season, nobody seemed to know who could and could not ride where. Running beside this new Conference League was the Youth Development League with four-man teams over six heats.

There were many more teams competing, seventeen in all, including several top teams such as Kings Lynn, Belle Vie, Sheffield and Glasgow. Mildenhall's four riders for this second-half league were mainly Mark Thompson, Jamie Barton, Simon Brown and Chris Sweet. There was a change of team manager when ex-rider Roger Horspool took on the duty.

There were a few other changes in workers at the track and Ray Maskall, who had been the starting marshall for some years, was succeeded by Graham Thompson who had an attractive assistant flag marshall in Alison Bateman, a welcome sight to any track; her father and two brothers also worked at West Row. On looking around on match days, it was seen that several faces on duty each meeting day were with the Fen Tigers right from the very beginning. It is also of interest in what paperwork was needed to be filled in and signed by various members of the track and management staff, including the referee who overlooks most of the activity during the meeting. He had the power to fine any wrongdoing and collect the fines on the day. He must sign in with his own time of arrival and receive paperwork from both team captains, machine examiner, Clerk of the Course and team captains. If any crashes occur and injury is also reported with a plan of the track and where it happened and then a medical officers report, helped by the tracks incident reporter; phew!, and you thought a referee's job is easy. I could also go into the reporting of track conditions, the nearest hospital and how many miles, and the rider's bikes, which must have certain things in order to allow them to race, but this could quickly fill an extra book on regulations, which seemed to change or updated as the head chiefs tell us, every year. Even riders helmets had to have an official stamp on them.

The Fen Tigers riders were much as the previous season with Geoff Powell back as captain. Dean Garrod had been wintering in New Zealand to help him with his racing career; Garry Sweet a solid middle order man, and Jamie Barton also keen to improve. Dean Chapman, a new young rider, was joined by 15-year-old Oliver Allen and a young Mark Thompson who was determined to get better with each new season. Allen rode just three league meetings before being taken back by Peterborough where he rode in the Premier League a few times. He later rode for Norfolk Braves on six occasions. Paul Lydes-Uings who had been signed from Arena Essex, while another returnee was Nathan Morton for the second successive season completing the squad. It was a very small Conference League this year consisting of just five teams, Buxton Hitmen, Newport Mavericks, Skegness Braves, St Austell Gulls and Mildenhall, and to try and provide more meetings the teams would face each other four times in the year -two home and two away

Mildenhall had a mixed start to the season, but things looked substandard in the early matches. To begin the league programme the Fen Tigers travelled to Newport on Good Friday for an eleven o'clock start, when it rained throughout the meeting, making condition rather unpleasant, but the team put on a good show but could not stop the powerful Welsh club winning 54-36 at Queensway. The Tigers provided just two heat winners in this meeting while two home riders recorded maximums. It could have been a lot closer had not Oliver Allen picking up an injury in his second ride. Geoff Powell reported a dreadful trip from his home in Cumbria and thought about turning back when he encountered heavy snow round Birmingham, but he battled on to do his useful work for the Tigers.

The first home meeting however was postponed because of the inclement weather. This was to have been a special match against Peterborough, a real local derby. The nightmare conditions led to another rain-off when Buxton Hitmen were due at West Row, but they made the journey again the following week to fulfil the fixture. The Fen Tigers all seemed to come together and wrapped up a big win 63-27. In his home debut, Oliver Allen registered a fifteen-point maximum, then going on to win the Rider of the Night in the second half. Ex Mildenhall Dave Jessup and new England team manager was on hand to present him with his trophy. Dean Garrod was on top form but in his last ride, he suffered a blown engine. Powell was in the wars with a frightening crash on the top bend with Phillip Knowles, leaving the Tigers captain bruised and the Buxton rider with stitches in a certain place, which hurt when sitting down. Impressive was the word for Dean Chapman who, after a first ride fall came good with two wins and a second.

The second home meeting was the Aquarius Stud Championship. This Stud was a business venture of old friend Malcolm Vasey and attracted some other team's riders such as England Under 21 international Paul Oughton, as well as nearly all the Mildenhall squad. Mildenhall's Oliver Allen won this individual meeting.

On the social side of things a properly formed Supporters Club was put in place, and many ideas were put forward to help raise much needed cash for riders, and the club itself. There were also to be coach trips arranged for each away meeting. This was the twenty-first season that the Fen Tigers had been in operation. The atmosphere at West Row had always been very special and more so when a visiting rider commented on the cheering loudly of every Mildenhall rider that made him rather nervous of riding here. A sponsored walk also took place from Burwell to Mildenhall in May. This raised £514 by those on the eleven-mile hike.

Next up was the visit of unbeaten Newport with old friend Maurice Morley, who goes back to the beginning of Mildenhall Speedway, in charge. He was an accomplished team manager who had also seen service at Exeter, Romford and Canterbury amongst other clubs. Newport had started up again and were going to bring along some good young riders to the sport. They went back to South Wales with the points and a 47-42 win. This fixture was a bit topsy-turvy as Mildenhall went eight points adrift midway and had to dig in to pull the scores level. Then they found themselves on the wrong end of a controversial decision when both the Tigers riders were excluded in heat thirteen; Oliver Allen and Geoff Powell being left to ponder on what the referee had found wrong when they were both hit by an opposing rider and were left sprawling on the track. Skipper Powell had just made a re-appearance after two weeks off with damaged ribs. The finest heat victory was that of young Thompson in the fourteenth, coming from way back to take the chequered flag.

The Fen Tigers then felt confident of some success, having won two challenge matches versus Skegness Braves, the Fen Trophy being revived once again. The seasiders arrived at West Row with two ex Mildenhall skippers in their line-up in Peter Boast and Simon

Wolstenholme, Peter showed he still knows the Mildenhall track very well with a fifteen-point maximum. A newcomer Bobby Eldridge, who had taken third place in the Aquarius Championship, started the season for Mildenhall and had quite an interesting debut against Skegness Braves in the home leg of the Fen Trophy. After blowing his engine up before the parade he had to borrow Simon Brown's; this did not stop him gathering up two wins in his tally of eleven points from number seven in the team. Powell also bent his bike when falling in the lead in the first heat and rode Darren Osborne's for the rest of the meeting. The Fen Tigers won both legs of the challenge.

When Simon Brown got his bike back for the second half it was not running very well at all. As it was needed for the next night at Skegness, it was all hands to the pumps. Simon spent most of the next night in his home workshop stripping the engine down to try to find the faults and by the time he put it together again it was early morning. Powell also had to borrow some spare parts for his bike to keep it on the go the next meeting. Eldridge was expected to have a very bright future in speedway, but just as suddenly announced his retirement after just a few weeks. The KO Cup had been re-introduced but this only meant at the most just two extra meetings, but the teams were given the nod to fix up more than the league matches.

On Sunday 31 May, there had been a fixture versus Arena Essex as a challenge match but as the Essex side had some problems getting a team together for this visit to West Row, a Conference Select team provided the Fen Tigers with the opposition to fill the Sunday date. Former Tiger Gavin Hedge captained this side made up with riders from Newport, Buxton and Peterborough, plus Phil Ambrose a young rider who was at the time engaged in his A-Levels. The meeting ended level at 45-45.

An eagerly looked forward to meeting, the Bernie Klatt Memorial Trophy was the next West Row date early in June with an Individual Meeting, the riders in the field being mainly those who had been connected with Mildenhall at times plus the seven current riders. Matt Read (Arena Essex) turned out the one to take home the top prize that included £150 and the trophy. He was just one point in front of Geoff Powell and Andrew Appleton (Newport) who had to run-off for second and third places, the Tigers captain settling for runners-up spoils.

The British weather resulted in the away meeting at Buxton Hitmen being called off, but not before most riders and people had arrived at the track. The heavens opened up before the time to start and although the track staff worked their socks off to get the racing on , and the start put off for one hour, it was eventually given up and all concerned made their damp way homewards.

Showing that the Mildenhall stadium was still a top for facilities the Qualifying Round of the Conference League Riders was staged next with riders from all the league clubs and Newcastle Diamonds and St Austell. Water caused the meeting to be held up at the start, but this was from a burst water-main close to the first bend which had to be sorted out as it came on to the track, but this was soon cured. Once again, Andrew Appleton showed his liking for the West Row track by ending in first place followed once again by Geoff Powell and Roger Lobb. Every one of the programmed riders turned up, which was a record in itself as individual meetings sometimes suffer from non-arrivals, and a wealth of reserve riders make up the numbers; at least it gives the younger ones a chance now and again. Other Mildenhall riders also had to try to qualify at other rounds at Newport, Skegness and St Austell.

When the cup match against Skegness came up the Fen Tigers looked odds on to reach the next stage having had two victories over their opponents already to start the season. The seaside town had started up the previous year but poor crowds had forced them to close and transfer to the Isle of Wight. But for 1998 'Uncle' Cyril Crane had come in to promote the new side, but things were not so much better. The track was a problem and affected the racing quality, and the team soon moved to share the Kings Lynn track for home meetings at Saddlebow Road.

While the Skegness Braves had trouble with their seaside racing track, they still had time to ring the praises over the Mildenhall stadium at West Row. Writing in their programme the well-named 'Skeggy' waxed lyrical about the Fen Tigers home, calling it 'marvellous' with great fish and chips, plus a bar and clubroom. Other promotions wanting to start up and build a stadium from scratch, were invited to go and have a look at the Mildenhall facilities and base their track on what had been achieved at West Row.

The Skegness team, now renamed the Norfolk Braves, was full of ex Tigers so a lot was expected of the cup match, or so said the media who talked up the meeting, helped no doubt by rival chairmen Dingle Brown and Cyril Crane. The first leg at West Row was to be followed in the same evening at Kings Lynn by the second leg. Oliver Allen the Mildenhall star youngster had been called up by Peterborough for their Premier League fixture, and as the Braves were a good man short in Gavin Hedge, both teams called on a junior rider to fill in, and this made the meeting sensibly close. As it was, there were a few exclusions during the match and the lead changing hands as well. For the visitors Peter Boast and Darren Smith were the top riders and the rules at that time led to Boast replacing one of the weaker riders in an important heat, then the Fen Tigers did the same bringing in Geoff Powell for young reserve Dean Chapman just afterwards. In the end, the Tigers came out on top by seven points 48-41, after some late heat wins. The main shock for Mildenhall was a telephone call to Dingle Brown from Bobby Eldridge saying he felt he had to give speedway a miss for a while owing to the finances and his work commitments. A search for a sponsor did not unearth any offers and he was not seen in the team any more that season.

Both teams then made a mad dash up the A10 for the second leg at Saddlebow Road, where the racing was just as thrilling with the Fen Tigers coming out victors 49-41 and overall by 97 to 82. The star in the second leg was Paul Lydes-Uings who rattled up fourteen from six rides, but Powell lost the race for the Bronze Helmet to Boast, from whom he had wrenched it in the afternoon at West Row. The Mildenhall seven were Geoff Powell, Dean Chapman, Gary Sweet, Mark Thompson, Chris Sweet, Dean Garrod and Paul Lyden-Uings.

After the meetings, there were many who stayed on including members of the Supporters Club, and darts became a favourite pastime in the clubroom and bar. As it was World Cup Football this year as well, the large screen was deployed when games were being beamed around the world, so fans of both sports did not feel left out. Highlights were a

Darts Match against the Rye House Supporters and a Grand Quiz Night. Supporters also had something else to celebrate when three Mildenhall riders got through to the Final of the Conference League Championship at St Austell in July; these being Dean Garrod, Paul Lydes-Uings and Jamie Barton. Powell's injured ankle forced him to withdraw from his last Qualifying Round. The British weather had a say in the Final, which was postponed until a later date.

The St Austell Gulls were visitors when Mildenhall were firing on all cylinders and the Tigers won 55-35. The only blot on the day was a £100 fine imposed on Nathan Morton in heat eight for what the referee called 'disorderly conduct'. After the main match, the Mildenhall Tiger Cubs met St Austell in the British Dunlop Development League but went down 26-10, winning just one heat through Chris Sweet. They had another outing after the following weeks meeting with Buxton with Eastbourne Eaglets the visiting team, The Cubs won this one 21-15 with the four of Mark Thompson, David Osborne, Simon Brown and Chris Sweet.

Meanwhile the Fen Tigers beat Buxton 49-41 in the first leg of the KO Cup semi-final with young Ross Brady, a new acquisition, putting up a score of thirteen plus a bonus in his first meeting, taking the place of Morton. He also raced for the Bronze Helmet losing out to Buxton's top scorer Simon Stead. Morton had crashed badly at Arena Essex dislocating his shoulder and kept in hospital overnight. The KO Cup meeting meant that a challenge match versus a Wolverhampton side had to be put off, and hoped to run this later on.

When Oliver Allen was also not available for Mildenhall in three meetings they had moved quickly to snap up Ross Brady who had been looking to sign for Skegness. He had soon showed his worth with a fantastic performance to help them to an impressive victory over the strong St Austell side 55-35 at West Row. Mildenhall then missed out when Skegness went out and persuaded Oliver Allen to join the seasider's, and he made his debut at the home meeting against - you have guessed it - the Fen Tigers. He put on the style with a fifteen point maximum as the Norfolk Braves turned out winners in the league fixture on 11 July by 51-38.In the Mildenhall side that night was Darren

-41-

Osborne, a late call-up for the absent Nathan Morton, and he weighed in with four hard won points in a meeting where rain fell throughout.

On their travels Mildenhall were not so successful and lost for the second time this season at Newport 56-34 and then at Skegness 51-38. The Development League team fared somewhat better when they went to Eastbourne winning 20-16 to complete the double over a strong Eagles team. Moreover, when the Skegness (re-named) Norfolk Braves came to West Row they juniors entertained the young Arena Essex riders the same night. Unfortunately, at 15-15 the last heat was not run owing to an injury to Mildenhall's Jamie Barton. The Cubs next match saw them lose to a Coventry side 23-13. Aiden Collins the son of ex rider Les Collins was in the Coventry team. In the Mildenhall loss to the Braves Ross Brady was again top scorer with fifteen points. After this setback against the Braves, the Fen Tigers then went out and handed out a rare defeat on the league leaders Newport Mavericks when they came to West Row 51-39.

In the replayed Riders Championship, the winner was Steve Bishop. Dean Garrod managed eight points and Paul Lydes-Uings four, Jamie Barton had also qualified but owing to his work commitments, he was unable to take his place in the field. With meeting each side four times this season and even more in the KO Cup, The Norfolk (ex Skegness) Braves and the Fen Tigers met eight times in this season. It seemed that every week old friends were turning up at West Row. The results continued to seesaw and had turned into losing away then winning at home. The Development team were doing well however and included another young new face in Adam Pryer for the first time.

When top-of-the-league St Austell visited Mildenhall for the second time in the league they nearly came off second best once again but held on to draw 45-45. It was interesting to note that in the list of top ten averages in the Conference League, there were three Fen Tigers and three St Austell. Making the long trek to Cornwall the Fen Tigers saw the meeting at St Austell curtailed after eleven heats with the scoreline at 46-20; the weather not being very helpful to the sport.

The Fen Tigers reached the final of the League KO Cup by beating

Buxton twice, by eight points at home and four points in Derbyshire. At one stage at Buxton, it seemed the chance had gone when Lydes-Uings fell heavily in heat two and had to withdraw from the meeting, but the other riders buckled down and obtained the result wanted. This was followed up when the young Cubs won their match versus Buxton as well. Ross Brady successfully defended the Bronze Helmet as well, so all round a good afternoon. The Meeting against the Braves on 23 August was a nightmare as with everything ready for the meeting it started to rain early in the afternoon. With all the riders present and St Johns Medics and the referee it was decided to wait for the rain to cease and then work on the track, and start at a later time. However, the rain did not play its part and became much worse and a track inspection revealed that no racing would take place that day and the meeting was cancelled.

They then had to face the formidable St Austell Gulls once again in the final; they were the league winners by this time. David Mason was in the Tigers line-up in place of Gary Sweet. The Gulls were too strong for the Tigers winning both legs and therefore completing the double. The Cornish side also provided the Conference League Riders Champions in Steve Bishop, their star rider, while another Gulls rider Seemond Stephens took third place.

The weather did not worry what havoc it caused and when an attractive meeting was arranged against a Swindon Select team at West Row it threatened once again but the match was run Mildenhall winning 53-37 with guest David Mason in the Mildenhall side. The last Development League meeting was against the Sheffield Prowlers. In the league Mildenhall finally finished in third place out of the five competitors

****

1999

With sponsorship coming to the fore, it was the Mildenhall 'Despatch Solutions' Fen Tigers when they took to the track. The line-up of riders for the new season was announced quite early in the year and was composed of Gary Sweet, Jitendra Duffil, Peter Johnson, Andrew Moore, Mark Blackwell, Gavin Hedge, Mark Thompson, Dean Garrod, and Barrie Evans. Hedge was returning to a former club and Moore was

-43-

a sixteen-year-old from Lincolnshire. One departure was Geoff Powell who decided to ride for his hometown club Workington, this was after his seven hundred round trips to Mildenhall each meeting last season, and he was a hard act to follow. One interesting event was the recording on Video of every Tigers meeting and which were then available to purchase by the supporters. The Fen Tigers were one of the first of the Conference League sides to take up this experience. Up to that time, it was only the top speedway teams who were doing this for their supporters.

However, it was still an undersized Conference League again, with just one more team than the previous year; competing were Kings Lynn Braves, Buxton Hitmen, Newport Mavericks, St Austell Gulls, Rye House and Mildenhall Fen Tigers. Somerset applied to join the Conference but then decided at the last moment to wait until next year; meanwhile Cradley Heath could have been in the league, which was what they had aimed for. The Development League was also running once again and the Tiger Cubs had their sponsor by Oakwood Publications. The Cubs were grouped with Reading, Oxford, Exeter, and Arena Essex. Once again, the clubs were looking around to fix in Challenge matches to keep the spectators happy and the riders on their toes. One such meeting involved Buxton who came to West Row for the opening meeting on 11 April, in what was titled the 'Fen/Dales Trophy. The Fen Tigers tracked two more new riders in this first fixture, Phillip Knowles was wearing the number one race jacket, after several months on the sidelines after a serious crash at West Row the previous year, and a battle had ensued behind the scenes with the chief's at Belle Vue before Knowles was a Mildenhall rider. At number two was Phil Ambrose a seventeen-year-old from Kent. Nevertheless, with the men from the hills winning both legs, of course the Fen Tigers shrugged it off as just to get some practice in.

When the real fixtures came along it also prompted the weather to intervene and the first league fixture versus Kings Lynn Braves was postponed. However, the return meeting the following evening at Kings Lynn took place with victory to the home team 50-39. The home meeting was re-arranged for two weeks ahead and while the racing did get underway, the rain descended once again and this time the meeting

-44-

was abandoned. In sunny weather the track was watered early on but with an hour to go the black clouds gathered over the stadium, the heavens opened and the track was very soon awash and after trying it everyone was in agreement that no proper racing could be done. Only three heats were run, as the Mildenhall line-up saw Gavin Hedge, Peter Johnson (from Berwick) and Simon Brown taking the places of Ambrose and Knowles, with Dean Garrod given the role of captain. A name from the past also re-joined the Fen Tigers when Maurice Morley phoned Dingle Brown and offered his services in any way to help the club along its way.

For the third meeting when St Austell Gulls visited the team was again re-shuffled, Sweet being at number one with his namesake Chris at two, Mark Thompson and the young Barrie Evans (a former mascot) in the reserve berths. It was Evans who top-scored with twelve points in his first ever match, but Mildenhall went down 48-42, the visiting team providing eleven race-winners to the home teams four. Two visits to Wales and the West brought two more losses at St Austell and Newport. Luck for the Tigers seemed to be against them as Gavin Hedge sustained a broken bone in his foot after a tangle with Stephens in the home match against St Austell, and did not make the long trips. Then at Newport Andrew Moore broke two ribs and a punctured lung when he crashed with Craig Gough, and spent a few days in hospital. Exams also meant Barrie Evans not available as well, while the St Austell meeting saw former grass-track rider Rickie Scarboro being brought in together with Simon Phillips who lives in Cornwall. With injuries not helping Mildenhall went out and signed Mark Blackwell from Workington.

Seven matches into the season and Mildenhall had still not registered a win, the losses including the first leg of the KO Cup against Kings Lynn, although it was at Kings Lynn and only one point between the teams 45-44. It was to prove a barnstormer of a meeting in the second leg at Mildenhall. With the Rye House Rockets starting up once again after their enforced break of five years, they were riding some of their home meetings at West Row, and started when the strong Linlithgow Lightning came to West Row; the Scottish outfit opposing Mildenhall first and then Rye House. For the Fen Tigers that day Garrod played a real captains part with sixteen points while Steve Camden came into the side at Reserve, and was doing fine until his engine blew. Mildenhall won 57-32, the first league win.

Along came the first of the challenge matches when Mildenhall entertained Club Cradley Heath, a side not seen too many times at the West Row stadium. After falling by the wayside the Heathens were taking part in Challenge matches all away from home, while their former headquarters and track stand idle; not a good situation. However, the supporters of the Black Country side have rallied round and are fighting hard to be able to return to their home very soon, but the principle of democracy is against them now but they are fighting to get their home back. After all the supporters just want to see their team return to their roots, and that like Rye House, both sides are playing away, in the proper sense of course.

Rye House put on four home league meetings, one knockout cup and a challenge match at West Row. There were some double-headers when the Tigers and Rockets race on the same night; quite a good arrangement for all the fans of both sides, especially when the opposing team are Newport who ride against both teams, Tigers and Rockets, which was the next date. The Rockets also rode a home meeting at Eastbourne and their home match versus Mildenhall at Kings Lynn. While the Rye House team was operating once again their track at Hoddesdon was deemed not up to scratch for staging speedway after the long enforced interruption

It was well into June but it was still only the Tigers fifth home meeting in the season; fixtures being very sparse at this time. Dean Garrod had taken over the captains roll but it was certainly not his day when he took a tumble in both his first two rides and was replaced in his remaining heats as he was carrying an injury. By now, Ricky Scarboro was in the side after deciding to try speedway after being a successful grass-track performer. Cradley Heath were the victors by 47-41 but Mildenhall made a fight of it, and after being behind for most of the match they suddenly sprung into gear and led by one point after heat twelve, only for the visitors to tussle back for the win. In the Cradley side was Phillip Knowles who was at Mildenhall at the beginning of the year.

-46-

The Tigers pair of Barrie Evans (14 + !) and Steve Camden (12) were certainly in form and it was through the efforts of these two that Mildenhall were able to keep close to their staunch visitors. Evans was the Fen Tigers mascot when a schoolboy, and was starting his riding career as a fifteen-year-old. He was soon taking some rides with Arena Essex a league higher; his second meeting with the Essex side seeing him notch up an impressive eleven points. The Norfolk teenager became the target for several clubs from the time he started to shine for the Fen Tigers. Steve Camden joined Mildenhall halfway through the season after being spotted trying out at Romney. He had previously been with Swindon Robins in the Elite League riding at reserve, but had not been riding so far in the current season. He made his Tigers debut in the win over Linlithgow and helped Mildenhall out of the rut they seemed to have settled into, his top score was twenty points from seven rides. He was a hard and exciting rider and had several clashes on and off the track with opposing riders of the same ilk. .

Injuries had taken their toll at Mildenhall and three riders were sitting it out on the sidelines, and when young Evans took a nasty tumble against Linlithgow, everyone held their breath but up popped the young lad and continued his excellent work for the team. It was going to prove hard to decide which riders to select when the limping wounded all return to fitness, but it was a beneficial thing to have, as it could be costly with not enough riders. Ex Mildenhall riders seemed to turn up everywhere and when the Newport Mavericks arrived at Mildenhall they had in their ranks a certain Bobby Eldridge.

The League KO Cup 2nd leg against Kings Lynn had been waiting for a few weeks but when it was finally run the Fen Tigers progressed to the next stage with a 52-38 victory, as the two reserves Evans and Camden totalled twenty-four points between them. Meanwhile the Braves were virtually a two-man team with thirty-three of their points coming from Freddie Stephenson and Darren Groves; they also borrowed Mark Thompson to make up their number. It was by now halfway through the season and the Fen Tigers had just one win to show for all their efforts in the league, but it was still a season to plan for the long term which the promoters were aiming for, and essential to keep speedway going each year at West Row. With injuries coming thick and fast promoter Dingle

Brown and his sidekick Malcolm Vasey were striving to make up a team for the semi-final of the KO Cup at St Austell. After missing since April, Phillip Knowles was again in the team, but Steve Camden knocked up seventeen points versus Buxton.

The most eventful meeting at the West Row Stadium for quite a few years was to be held on Saturday 14 August when the Conference League Riders Championship came to the Fens. This was the special night for the top riders from each Conference team and this yearly meeting attracted supporters of all the League teams, plus others who just love speedway and a high-quality list of riders. There was a smattering of riders with Mildenhall connections in the star-studded entry list. Ex captain Simon Wolstenholme (with Rye House) another captain Peter Boast (Kings Lynn), Phillip Knowles and Bobby Eldridge who had both ridden for the Fen Tigers in the current year, Jonathan Swales (Linlithgow), and of course the Mildenhall hopefuls Gary Sweet, Barrie Evans and Steve Camden. The champion for 1999 was Jonathan Swales with Steve Camden runner-up and Scott Courtney third. Appleton was striving for a top three finish when in the last heat he tried a mite too hard and was excluded for unfair riding when he brought down Steve Camden.

After the trip to Cornwall in the KO Cup Mildenhall surprised many folk by travelling up to Scotland a few days later and won 45-44 at Linlithgow. On the trip north some fans also took in a meeting at Edinburgh where Ross Brady is now riding in the Premier League. The next day Shane Colvin made his debut, as did Jitenndra Duffill, both continuing in the team against a League Select team the next week. The Fen Tigers finished the season with a flourish as their last five home meetings produced a draw (v St Austell in the KO Cup) and four victories over a League Select, Arena Essex, Kings Lynn and Rye House. With two heat-leaders out injured for the Kings Lynn visit - Sweet and Camden - the Tigers tracked Lee Dixon in the team, who did well for three second places and three bonus points.

For their final away meeting in the league the Fen Tigers faced Rye House at Kings Lynn where they were not allowed to use rider-replacement although the two heat-leaders were still missing through injury. Instead, they were forced to nominate a reserve rider, David Osborn, who was not present and had not known he would be required in the mix-up. As a result Mildenhall could only put one rider out in some heats and it was to their credit they only went down by ten points (40-50). The meeting versus Arena Essex Select also included the British Development League versus Eastbourne Eaglets and followed by Rye House against Newport; altogether thirty-six heats of speedway.

Altogether, Mildenhall used eighteen different riders through the season. On the final meeting versus Rye House the Tiger Cubs had a match against Reading Ravens, also some demonstration rides with some 1920 bikes and ex riders, plus another heat of classic bikes, which saw ex Fen Tiger Derek Harrison on a Weslake. In a season which had promised much but delivered little, due to the weather and injuries, the race night had been moved to Saturday to attract more followers, but as the promoters commented "If we had been the only team in the league we probably would not have won it." They did however avoid the bottom place but only because of their late winning streak

****

2000

The Millennium season saw the league keeping its name for a change, and as the Conference League, it also stuck to the fifteen-heat formula to try to standardise the approach to speedway. Clubs had increased to ten and a bonus system was put in operation for aggregate wins over the two league matches between the clubs, and there was to be a League Cup as well as the KO Cup. Six members of the Fen Tigers side, which ended the 1999 season, were back at West Row with Paul Lydes-Uings returning to the ranks to take the place of Gary Sweet who decided to move to Rye House.

Much was hoped from Steve Camden who pledged himself to the Tigers after coming into the side in June 1999, and had spent highly on his machine for the coming campaign. Phillip Knowles faced a long journey from Bradford but chose to ride for Mildenhall, while eighteen-year-old Shane Colvin was doubling up with Reading Racers in the Premier League, having averaged eight from his four outings for Mildenhall the previous year. Jitendra Duffil was combining a University course with his speedway career and hailed from Teeside,

(5) STEVE CAMDEN

(6 top) SIMON WOLSTENHULME
(6 bottom) MILDENHALL 2001

(7) MILDENHALL FEN TIGERS

Back Row: L to r - Darren Andrews, Wayne Broadhurst, Paul Lydes-Uings, Matthew Wright, Mark Thompson.
Front row - Thomas Allen, Gavin Hedge, Scott James.

(8 top) v Buxtonl. l to r LEE HODGSON (blue) JAMES MANN
(yellow/black) WAYNE BROAD HURST (red)
(8 bottom) MILDENHALL TEAM 2002

(9 top) PAUL LEE
(9 bottom) FEN TIGERS 2004

(10) PAUL LEE

and the terrific youngster Barrie Evans was eager to start racing once again. It was one of the youngest sides that Mildenhall had tracked. One other change was that Rye House had finally moved back to their proper home at Hoddesdon again.

It was still the same promoters and management headed by Dingle Brown, and Gavin Hedge - son of Trevor - was appointed captain. There were changes to the programme with a strikingly front cover, and the race jackets were re-designed. Promoter Dingle Brown also turned up with a new car, although this was needed after his Ford Granada blew up just before the start of the season. His van also suffered a broken bearing in a wheel so that had to be quickly fixed, but he was back in operation just in time for the opening meeting.

The newly formed Boston Barracuda-Braves were the visitors to Mildenhall for the opening meeting of the new season, in the now legendary Fen Trophy. Some of their riders had ridden for Mildenhall in the past including Peter Boast and Dean Garrod in recent times, and Robert Hollingworth who spent one season at West Row in the middle eighties. Having won the away leg of this trophy by two points, the Tigers then proceeded to run away in the home leg and ended up with a 58-32 victory and 103-75 overall.. Camden, Hedge and Evans chalked up double figures while nine points came from Jitendra Duffil. In the away leg at Kings Lynn David Osborne came into the side scoring three and which would have been more had he not been on the wrong end of some refereeing decisions.

A Challenge match came next against Peterborough Puma's who had also been resurrected and joined the Conference League to provide Mildenhall another local derby meeting as in the old days. This meeting was also Barrie Evans sixteenth birthday which he promptly celebrated by top-scoring with a paid maximum (14 + 1) as the Fen Tigers won easily 66-24. In this meeting, there was a rather horrific crash involving Lydes-Uings and the visitors Pryer and a spontaneous collection amongst the fans produced over two hundred pounds for Paul's bike to be repaired, which had suffered more damage than both riders had. In addition, in the Puma's line-up were two figures who were due to play a part in the Mildenhall history in the future, Jason King and Chris

Schramm; they were the top scorers for Peterborough.

Then came the first home league meeting and a victory over Sheffield at West Row 51-39.This meeting was also the debut for another Fen Tigers protégé in Matt Thompson who proceeded to score a second place in his very first ride. Sheffield's Adam Allot was following in the family tradition of Uncle Tommy, Grandad Guy and Father Nicky. The first leg of the League Cup versus Rye House followed this, but the second leg that was to follow the next day had already been postponed until a later date. Len Silver and his merry band of track staff had been working hard on the new track surface but were not ready for the opening and 15 May was the date decided upon, Mildenhall's visit to Hoddesdon being sometime in the future. It was Shane Colvin who led the way versus Rye House at West Row, with a fine fifteen-point maximum while for Rye House David Mason was on form scoring fourteen for his team, Mildenhall ending on top 53-37. The Bronze Helmet was in operation once again this year and in this run-off, David Mason was the winner over the Fen Tigers Shane Colvin.

The Supporters Club at Mildenhall was going from strength to strength with membership at £5 and a Junior Branch for £2-50. The younger ones have a free draw each week and a chance to meet their favourite riders, and competitions along the way such as a drawing of their top riders. For the 'grown-ups' there was always the coach trips to away meetings and dart matches against rival Supporters Clubs in the bar after the meetings. A new addition to the sales this year was a Fen Tigers wristwatch with the clubs logo, and costing £22, and included a lifetime guarantee and was waterproof. I wonder if anyone still has one of these. Another team was the dedicated track staff at West Row who at times had to work nearly through the night after the Saturday meetings of Stock Cars. One such family were on holiday at Great Yarmouth one week-end but still turned up bright and early on the Sunday to help put up the safety fence, side-by-side with Dingle and son Simon.

Mildenhall had started the season like an express train and the title looked as if it was in the Fen Tigers hands again if the start was anything to go by. Some fine home wins were registered and a run of seven successive wins was put together before the sequence ended with a defeat (49-40) at Linlithgow in Scotland. Missing Steve Camden owing to work the Fen Tigers put up a good show with captain Gavin Hedge leading the way. The Mildenhall management had ridden under protest as the insisted the Scottish side used an illegal rider and would have to wait for the outcome of this. However, after postponed meetings at West Row against St Austell and the return in Cornwall due to heavy rain, the Fen Tigers promptly had their revenge when Linlithgow came to Mildenhall, and were sent home after a loss by 57-33. Steve Camden and Barrie Evans both scored seventeen points and Phillip Knowles also in double figures.

At the beginning of June the Fen Tigers took in three matches in six days, at St Austell, Newport and Sheffield, and which started with a fine win in Cornwall 55-35. When the trip to Newport came along it was this, which could decide if the Fen Tigers were worthy title challengers, or not. The Mavericks were the reigning league champions, but for the trip to Wales Barry Evans was on the injured list as they rode rider replacement. While two of last years Newport side had moved up a league, they had replaced them with equally good riders, one being new Aussie discovery Lee Herne. The first heat went 5-1 to the visitors but the next heat was a reverse by 5-0 as both Tigers fell. Taking his riders-replacement ride in the third heat Steve Camden suffered an exclusion and some thought the Tigers bubble had burst. Paul 'Butch' Lydes-Uings then got to work from the reserve berth, where he had been prolific since returning to Mildenhall after a year out of the saddle. Ending with two maximum heat wins the Fen Tigers took the points by 48-41. Paul top scored with 16+2 and Shane Colvin with 12+1. The full side was Steve Camden, Phil Knowles, Barrie Evans (RR), Gavin Hedge, Shane Colvin, Paul Lydes-Uings and Jitendra Duffill. This was the first defeat at home for Newport since 1998.

If this was not enough the trip to Sheffield was the hardest and Mildenhall lost 50-40 but did earn the bonus point, by 91-89. This was despite being without Evans who was required by Arena Essex and Colvin out of action with a bad injury to his toe. Ian Leverington stood by as a reserve rider for these three away meetings much to the relief of team manager Brown. Mildenhall were now more or less - excluding injuries - fielding a settled seven riders and it showed in the team spirit at that time. Evans had joined Arena Essex permanently and to cover this for the immediate future it was decided to have rider-replacement. They had a slice of luck when a loss at Ashfield was overturned when it was found Linlithgow had tracked Rusty Harrison, who was not eligible, and taking away his points the win went to the Tigers. A first title since 1979 looked very much on the cards.

The meeting on 18 June Mildenhall v Peterborough Pumas, looked to be a test for the Mildenhall side with both Evans and Camden missing for Mildenhall but the visitors were virtually a three-man team with Ian Barney, Derek Harrison & Adam Pryer scoring all but two of their point's total. A young rider James Horton had been having some time on track at Peterbro and Mildenhall lately and when he turned fifteen and went into the Pumas side at number two, The Fen Tigers stormed to a 54-36 victory with young Mark Thompson coming in at number one and winning his first race. The bond between supporters and riders at Mildenhall showed itself when a man walked into the pits after the meeting and gave all concerned a bonus for their win.

The home meeting with the new Somerset side was a real thriller with a last heat decider, and this after Mildenhall had lost the opening heat 5-0. The final score? 45-44 to the Fen Tigers. With Phillip Knowles unavailable for a few weeks, young Matt Thompson was given a run in the team. A Challenge match saw Cradley Heath visit Mildenhall for the second season running; they were being kept going by a band of supporters who hoping to get back to their stadium in the Black Country very soon. Of interest was a very young James Brundell who had some runs around the West Row track during the intervals.

Rye House were the opposition in the KO Cup semi-final, but the Fen Tigers were only able to register a narrow 48-42 win in their home leg and it looked to be a tight affair in the second leg at Rye House. The Monday night clash at Rye House in the second leg of the League Cup saw Mildenhall go down 47-41, as their rivals took the honours for this season. Nearly all the Tigers riders had a fall in this meeting as they struggled to come to terms with the tricky track conditions. The string of misfortunes started in heat one when Steve Camden caught the rear of an opponents bike from the tales and fell quite lightly but was soon found to have broken his wrist. The rest of the team plugged away but with engine failures and innocent falls not helping at all. The next away meeting at Peterborough was going along nicely for Mildenhall and by heat ten, they were comfortably eight points in the lead. Then the rains came, and how! In addition, the meeting was literarily washed out, as the track very soon resembled a river as everyone watched from the shelter of the grandstand and pits.

The Cup matches were followings quickly and it was a quick return for Somerset in the League Cup semi-final second leg on 16 July, their captain being Simon Phillips who had a few outings with the Fen Tigers the previous season. The Tigers were on top form however and won 54-34. As the Fen Tigers had lost down at Somerset by just 46-43, they were the League Cup winners, the first Mildenhall success for several years and a nice piece of silverware to display in the clubroom and bar. Both legs of this final were said by many who were there to have been a fine advert for Conference League moral with both sets of riders giving their all

The home and away meetings with Buxton Hitmen saw four more points added to the Mildenhall total, a win at West Row and a draw in the Peak District, plus the bonus point. Incidentally in the home match versus Buxton a lady rider, Charley Kirtland had an outing in the second half, and did very well in her races; a touch of the future? The finishing straight was now in sight with six more league fixtures to go. To keep everyone on their toes a challenge meeting saw Southampton visit the Tigers. The Saints are pressing their local council for a new home after a lapse of many years for this club. Meanwhile the Essex Junior Championship took place at Arena Essex and three of the riders in the final were from Mildenhall, Shane Colvin, Barrie Evans and Gavin Hedge, but they filled the runners-up places, as Luke Clifton was the overall winner.

However a shock came when Shane Colvin, who had been Mildenhall's rider at the CLRC at Newport, surprisingly announced he was going to move to Wales and ride for the Newport side. He had been in double figures for most of his seventeen meetings with the Tigers and his unanticipated decision came just hours before an important visit to

Boston that the Tigers then lost by a wide margin (57-33) although Darren Pearson was brought in as a replacement. An injury suffered in Holland by Paul Lydes-Uings also kept him out of the team. Tom Rowlett was also borrowed and took a surprise win in his first race when he shot from the gate to lead the home pair from start to finish. This Boston victory was their first of the season over Mildenhall after losing the first four matches to the Fen Tigers.

The return fixture was won by Mildenhall led by newcomer Pearson with fifteen plus two, despite a fall in one heat, and Barry Evans also with fifteen points; Pearson also took the Man of the Match award, a decision that was cheered by the large crowd, but the bonus point went to Boston. There was a painful twist in the tail for the Tigers when Steve Camden came off heavily in the last heat and was taken by ambulance off the track. This win was thought to have etched the Mildenhall name of the League Trophy, and made near certain when they trounced Newport, the reigning champions two weeks later 59-31

The season ended in great controversy and in the end, it was the home meeting versus St Austell, which lost Mildenhall the league title. It had been rained off in May, and despite the efforts to restage this on several occasions time ran out after the 28 October meeting versus the Cornwall side was again washed out, and although the Fen Tigers were awarded the bonus point, the match was not allowed to be staged out of season - said the BSPA. Dingle Brown the Mildenhall manager also pointed out that twenty-one years previously the Fen Tigers had won the League with victory in their last match at Scunthorpe on 4 November 1979; out of season. So finishing level with Sheffield who had completed all of their matches; and having notched more match points than Mildenhall - which of course they had raced one more meetings than Mildenhall - the Yorkshire club were crowned champions to some amazement at West Row and also many other teams over the country. It is of interest that although the Yorkshire outfit had chalked up more match points than the Fen Tigers, on the other side Sheffield had leaked twenty-two more points against them than Mildenhall.

So again, Mildenhall fell foul of the Speedway bosses who had once again put the country upstarts in their place with a strict application of the rules, which seemed to change every year. It was a real kick in the teeth for Dingle Brown who had himself taken many knocks in his involvement in speedway as a rider and promoter. An appeal was lodged to no avail and to add insult to injury he was fined £100 for not running the meeting, which he was prevented from doing by the speedway 'Gods', and refusing to let Mildenhall run the postponed meeting on 1 November. Nevertheless, just up the road at Kings Lynn ran their last meeting on that self same night in the Elite League.

To top it all St Austell made it known that they were quite willing to travel to Mildenhall on 4 November to get the fixture completed. A disillusioned Brown declared "I have had our supporters ringing me up literally in tears, and they can't understand what has happened; how do you explain a thing like this to them." The Conference League championship trophy was also in Dingle's house, having been forwarded to him from last season's winners Newport, who must have thought that was where it should be this year. Mildenhall had always backed up the SCB and the BSPA and took part in the leagues, whatever they were called and even when the number of teams involved was nearly down to nil. Although the Conference League title was morally the Fen Tigers they were prevented to celebrate and some riders in their career would not have this chance of a medal again, and that was the most unwarranted end to a very good season.

****

2001

The Conference League was still failing to attract clubs to its ranks and operated for the 2001 season with the usual names on board; Peterborough, Boston, Somerset, Newport, Buxton, Rye House and Sheffield. However, the Trophy was run on a mini-league basis, plus the KO Cup giving a few more meetings. To start the season a three-team tournament was arranged between Mildenhall, Peterborough and Boston, while Rye House provided the opposition in a home and away match dubbed the Spring Cup; these before the official league meetings began. Mildenhall were hopeful of fielding most of last season riders with the notable exception of young Barrie Evans who had joined Arena Essex in the Premier League. Most of the riders had a day at Kings Lynn to sort out the bikes and a practice session. New rules for the Conference League included the 'Golden Double' in tactical substitutions, the rider brought in to start fifteen metres back from the tapes, but his points count as double to the final score. With Roger Horspool as team manager, wife Vickie was also involved in helping to run the Supporters Club. For the supporters this meeting saw the Barber's Track Shop on the main terracing for the first season.

The season proper started with the Peterborough leg of the three-team tournament and the Fen Tigers came second ten points behind the hosts. The gremlins struck early and Darren Pearson and Phillip Knowles suffered some problems that affected the outcome. After the meeting at Peterborough Jitendra Duffil said that he was most likely to be giving up speedway as the harder he tried the worse things were getting. The Boston leg of this tournament was rained off with the home Tigers leg to come.

With the League ruling a mite misty on the inclusion of certain riders, Rye House took advantage to include both David Mason and Simon Wolstenholme - experienced riders - in their team for the visit to West Row for the first meeting of 2001. All clubs were waiting for the authorities to sort out this particular rule and come up with the right answer. In the Mildenhall team for the first time was seventeen-year-old Steve Clarke, while Dingle Brown was hot on the trail of another experienced rider to join Mildenhall. The visitor's side was packed with ex-Tigers but of these Phil Ambrose and Gary Sweet took no further part in the meeting when they were injured in their first rides of the afternoon, but the match went to the last heat when Wolstenholme and Mason took a 5-1 to give Rye House the victory 47-41. All this after they had managed to put out only one rider in three of the heats One unwelcome visitor for the opening meeting at West Row was the clouds of dust throughout the meeting, and no amount of watering could stop this on the day. The second leg of this Spring Cup was also won by Rye House on their own track 59-31. Gavin Hedge suffering a dislocated shoulder in a fall. In fact two falls in the same heat, which saw a trip to the ambulance and two attempts to put it back in place until a Paramedic from the crowd turned up and did the job straightaway; apart from this he injured one of his fingers quite severely as well. As it was, Hedge was out of action for several weeks.

-57-

The experienced rider mentioned as being signed for Mildenhall turned out to be Malcolm Simmons but this had to be put on hold as the BSPA classed him and Steve Camden as 'old hands' and therefore could not be used together in the same team, and a definite ruling by 'them that rule' was looked for, but until then? Pushed into a meeting at Rugby the BSPA lifted the 'old hand' restriction on Steve Camden that left the Fen Tigers with no old hand in their team at all, but the Simmons story had by now faded.

The visit of Peterborough was looked forward to as they looked on paper to have one of the strongest line-ups in the League. But it turned out they were more of just a two-men side, Ian Barney and Chris Schramm scoring nearly two thirds of their teams total as they went down to the Fen Tigers 48-41 in the first Conference League fixture. Phil Knowles was top points man for Mildenhall with twelve from a reserve berth, while a surprise inclusion was Barrie Evans who notched up eleven points. Thomas Rowlett also came into the Tigers team

The next two weeks turned out to be a mixed bag of fortune when a fine home win over Buxton 65-25 in the League Trophy, was followed by a not so good result at Newport A trip to the Peak District however saw the Fen Tigers winning at Buxton 46-44. It was level at 42 each going into the last heat. Paul Lydes-Uings and Phil Knowles were the two Tigers who took a 4-2 to take the points. Mildenhall had to borrow a young Karl Mason to fill their reserve position. It was a far from strong Mildenhall team which rode against Somerset at West Row and they went under 52-37 Another spanner was thrown into the works when Mark Thompson decided he could not afford to carry on racing; this after he had blown an engine and then crashed on Thomas Rowlett's bike which he also badly damaged. Matt also failed to score in the home meeting versus Somerset. One good thing was the sight of skipper Gavin Hedge having a second half ride in this meeting, after some time on the injured list.

The final leg of the three-team tournament was finally run at Boston (Kings Lynn) and the Fen Tigers came out the winners with an aggregate score of 110 points over the three meetings. Most of the early fixtures were in the League Trophy, which gave the Fen Tigers a chance to sort out their side in time for the League meetings. It was well into July before the Trophy was finished and Mildenhall had only raced two league meetings up to then (one lost and one won).

The meeting at West Row against Boston on Sunday 17 June was also to include the Ivor Hughes Memorial Trophy on behalf of the Cradley Heath supporters. Hughes was a young Cradley rider with a brilliant future when he was killed in a track accident in 1966. The British weather had a final say in this and the meeting had to be cancelled as the rain came down once again. Off the track, three Fen Tigers went to the local Littleport Show with their bikes and gave a demonstration in the main ring to spread the news of speedway in East Anglia.

The two meetings in the Trophy against Rye House proved very close and both sides won 47-43 on their own tracks, so a run-off for the bonus point saw Mildenhall take this, when seventeen-year-old Barrie Evans inflicted the first defeat that afternoon on Rye House's David Mason. For the League KO Cup Mildenhall faced Peterborough home and away in early June, and keeping the scoreline to within four points at the Showground the Fen Tigers won their way to the next round with a victory 54-36 at home two days later. The Bronze Helmet was up for grabs at the home meeting with the Puma's and Barrie Evans took this away from Ian Barney in great style.

The Mildenhall team manager Roger Horspool did not exactly gain favours with the home supporters at Peterborough when he asked the poor track to be re-graded, and this only after two Peterborough riders had crashed. Boos from the crowd saw the referee take a look and decide to carry on with the meeting, as there was a ten o'clock curfew. He had his work to do in the second leg at West Row when the Peterborough team manager tried a fast one to put his rider in as a 'Golden Double' until it was pointed out this only counted in League meetings and not any Cup action

Having a ride after the recent meetings was a familiar figure in blue leathers, no other than Carl Baldwin, a blast from the past; also trying out the Mildenhall track was a young Australian Nigel Sadler currently with Peterborough's Elite squad. The rain that caused the Boston meeting to be put off also saw the World Champions Mark Loram a chance to try out a new machine at Mildenhall.

The last League Trophy meeting was the home fixture against Boston Barracuda Braves, which Boston won 45-43, leaving Mildenhall nowhere near qualifying. It could be blamed on the gremlins getting to the home bikes once again, and at one time, everyone was lending machinery to other riders and one completely blasted engine lying on the pit floor. The second half racing after the Boston match came to a swift close when three riders crashed heavily, Simon Brown, Ian Leverington and Rob Painter; no bones broken but many bruises and tangled machinery.

Then it was on to the League proper and only the second home league match of the year against Somerset Rebels. This started in dramatic fashion when Mildenhall lost the first two heats by 5-1 and never really recovered and went down 50-4 after never in the lead, to one of the stronger teams in the Conference League.

The Tigers then paid a second visit to Somerset, a team they had faced three meetings in a row. Moreover, lost all three. This losing streak then extended to four when Boston were the winners at Kings Lynn. Mildenhall riders were not quite finished with Somerset as two, Steve Camden and Paul Lydes-Uings made the same journey for their away Round of the Qualifying Riders Championship; Gavin Hedge had a shorter trip for his away round at Rye House, as did Barrie Evans at Kings Lynn.

The Fen Tigers were on a most unwelcome losing run when Newport came to visit West Row, and Mildenhall picked this one out to register a most welcome victory 49-41. For the Tigers both Camden and Hedge scored twelve points, and the homesters were never behind in this meeting. A good crop of riders were appearing in the second half at West Row; Chris Mills, Carl Downs, Matthew Wright, Luke Bowen and a young woman Jessica Lamb, trying her luck.

The Mildenhall round of the Conference League Riders Championship caused some confusion during the month of August; the original date of the twelfth with a fine line-up was postponed because of bad weather, and then the restaging date fell to the same fate. At last, it could be run on 26 August when David Mason was the meetings winner, but the field looked nothing like the original list of riders. One ex Mildenhall rider was most welcome, this being former Fen Tiger Kevin Teager, who was at one of the August meetings; he suffered a career ending injury a few seasons previously.

It was away from West Row that the Fen Tigers were certainly not firing on all fronts and for the third time this season the opposition piled up over sixty points against Mildenhall. This time it was old friends and rivals Rye House who put the Tigers to the sword 63-27. However, the following home meeting against Buxton was a win for the Tigers by 47-43. This lifted them off the bottom of the league, but it took a last heat decider to give the Tigers the points. Captain Gavin Hedge showed great determination by turning out when suffering from the 'flu and also a poisoned hand. Having Steve Camden on the injured list again did not help matters especially in the Mildenhall away meetings. After the main match the competition run by the Supporters Club was decided; this was how far a speedway bike could go on a litre of fuel (eleven and three-quarter laps). Former rider Geoff Powell was the man on the machine and the winner of the £50 prize was Russell Avis from Newmarket. While it was nice to see Geoff back at West Row he said he was definitely retired from speedway as he was entering the marriage stakes very shortly. The following Sunday Mildenhall gained their revenge of Rye House with a very close 46-44 victory, despite the excellent eighteen point maximum from Rye House David Mason.

It was Gavin Hedge and Barrie Evans who represented Mildenhall in the Conference League Riders Championship at Rye House on 8 September, and the winner turned out to be David Mason, who had also come out top in the Mildenhall Qualifying Round. The two Fen Tigers were off the pace a bit and as Rye House was not their most favourite track at the best of times they were only in mid-table with the scores.

Up next for the Fen Tigers was the League KO Cup semi-final against Somerset. Losing by twenty points after the away meeting, Mildenhall then proceeded to lose by the same score at home (55-35). Steve

Camden was back in action for the Somerset away match and promptly saw his clutch disintegrate causing something like £700 amount of damage. Lydes-Uing was also in the wars and ended his season prematurely, while in the lead in two heats Hedge had his engine cut-out; investigations later found that a big spider was in the carburettor; whatever next?

During the season Dingle Brown finally got his man when Scott Courtney joined Mildenhall, having been riding with Premier League Glasgow. He turned in an average of 5.52 in his five outings for the Fen Tigers but when the new management team took over at West Row the next season he was overlooked and joined Rye House for 2002. Riding against Mildenhall in 2002 he announced his retirement from the sport, at least for a time.

For the visit of the strong Sheffield Prowlers Steve Camden showed how he had been missed through injury as he notched up fifteen points for Mildenhall, but hey again went down at home 47-41. Five Fen Tigers falling when well placed did not help matters either. The Fen Tigers went into their last home match of the season trailing a run of four defeats, and to add to their woes they had to put on their finale versus Boston at Rye House. The original date of 21 October was rained off and this left no dates available to re-stage this match due to the Stockcars and Greyhounds having the stadium booked as one of their dates of operation. Boston inflicted another loss on the Fen Tigers who were sadly well below strength with Cael Downs at number one for Steve Camden, Chris Geer taking the place of Knowles and Edward Kennett also coming into the team. The last named did great with eleven points and Barrie Evans top scoring with thirteen.

There was no consistency in the team's performances and they finished way down in the league table. It was thought by many that some Conference League sides line-ups were being changed weekly by some teams, mainly for the better, and with Mildenhall riders having to honour work commitments at various times during the year, it was chop and change on a regular basis. There was a change of venue for the end-of-season Presentation Evening, the Soham By-Pass Hotel being chosen this year, taking place on 3 November, where the supporters can forget about the awful season and look forward to things changing for the better next year.

****

2002

The threat of closing down once again shadowed Mildenhall as the beginning of a new season got nearer; promoter Dingle Brown said he was not able to run the club any longer, this after close on a decade at the mast head of HMS Mildenhall. The Fen Tigers owe a great deal to Dingle as but for his hard work and enthusiasm, Mildenhall would not have survived the previous years of the 1990's. The outgoing promotion certainly left a firm foundation and a superb pedigree for the future the Fen Tigers. Nevertheless, in stepped Tony Mole to buy the club just in time, then bringing in ex speedway rider Graham Drury to run the club for him. Graham's wife Denise was also an important cog in the West Row operation while Michael Lee was brought into the set-up, and the experienced Peter Thorogood climbed aboard as the track curator.

There were also some new faces in the riders, Wayne Broadhurst being the new number one, Scott Lamb another newcomer from Adelaide, South Australia, and who is based in Scotland, Mark Thompson returning, plus Thomas Allen. From the last season were Gavin Hedge, Paul Lydes-Uing and Thomas Rowlett. Of the previous seasons riders Barrie Evans had signed for Rye House while taking rides in the Premier League, and Steve Camden moved to Boston. Steve had bad luck with his new team, breaking his thumb in his first meeting. All teams were limited to using at any one time more than four riders with a Conference average at the beginning of the season, of more than 5.0 points. The two lowest average riders were assessed by the BSPA and could only ride at reserve. Mildenhall also took part in a Southern Junior League for second half's against the likes of juniors from Reading, Rye House, Eastbourne and Wimbledon.

The Conference League was now greatly increasing in numbers, twelve clubs now in operation including newcomers Carmarthen (a completely new club), Kings Lynn, Newcastle and Wimbledon (after eleven years out of the action). There were also the Trophy meetings, again in a mini-league basis, and competing just in these matches were

-63-

Swindon, and Wolverhampton. This competition began life two seasons back as the Conference League Cup. Somerset were not contesting the league this season. Together with the League KO Cup, there would be a minimum of thirty-three meetings plus any challenge matches that could be arranged; the most Mildenhall had contested for several years. Of interest, only Buxton and Mildenhall have been ever presents in the Conference League. Two semi-finals and the final would decide the League Riders Championship, and the Bronze Helmet made yet another return to be raced at league matches only

This partnership got off to a wonderful start with a string of wins, including the first three away meetings; at Newcastle and Boston in the league and a Trophy victory at Swindon. Scott James made an impressive debut for the Tigers at Newcastle. Then the weather had a say in what was happening and the first home meeting, a challenge match versus Wimbledon was rained-off. This was a big disappointment as the great Ronnie Moore MBE was travelling with the 'Dons. Several members of the Mildenhall League winning side also came along and all was doing well until just before the start when the rain came down and it was impossible to run the meeting. It was a comeback for the Wimbledon team as they had been missing from the scene for eleven tears. An early-published league table placed Peterborough way out at the top, although they already had six meetings, more than they already had anyone else; Mildenhall were seen in fourth place with two wins from two matches.

One of the changes at the West Row stadium was the charge for the car park where up to then it had been free. However, with a new kind of air safety fence erected as directed by the SCB, the new promotion team was determined to not starting to run at a loss which sometimes had been the case in the past. There was a hint of how the team was to be run, this meaning to have a squad system, as some occasions riders were to be unavailable for various reasons. This was shown in the home meeting with Boston Braves when Mark Thompson stood down to allow Heath Robinson to have an outing. Mildenhall duly won their first home meeting 49-41.

There was a different reason for the home meeting against the brand new club from Wales Carmarthen to be postponed; this was that the promotion was not quite satisfied with the new air fence that had been erected. Colin Meredith of the BSPA came in at our request to design and build a safety fence which will be the best around. Safety was always to the fore and especially at that time as just two weeks previous David Nix had lost his life while riding in the match Kings Lynn versus Newcastle Gems A planned visit to Sheffield was also rained off, as the season was beginning to be an on and off affair. Already Gavin Hedge had benefited from the good form shown for the Fen Tigers and had been given a ride in the Premier League with Reading this was one of the aims of the Mildenhall club as it had been ever since the beginning in the 1970's. Gavin impressed so much he was asked to join them, which he did, but he would remain a Mildenhall asset. Scott James was also riding for Workington and it was an injury while with them at Stoke that had sidelined him early in the season. It was with Workington that Mark Thompson was given some Premier League experience as well.

Correspondents in the Speedway publications had already taken a hard look at Mildenhall and liked what they saw, and commented on what was called a 'protective shield' of five riders all capable of being heat leaders, and the capture of Scott Lamb was a major surprise, but only four of their top riders can ride at the same time. The Fen Tigers were also tipped as the possible winners of the League, even at this early stage with a long season ahead, and they were unbeaten. This did not last long as the visit to Sheffield for the re-staged meeting, which was rained-off, saw the Steel City riders inflict the first reverse 48-42 in the Fen Tigers. This despite the Fen Tigers providing ten of the heat winners on the night. The one Mildenhall rider who stood out like a beacon on the night was Mark Thompson who deserved every point the made, sometimes coming from the back. In his third season with the Fen Tigers Paul Lydes-Uing was given the role of captain when Hedge was riding for Reading who were short of riders, but was still in the Fen Tigers plans. Paul's comment was "The way I see it, I want to turn up at a meeting and meet with six friends."

The long looked for meeting at West Row with long term rivals Peterborough then went the way of numerous speedway meetings in this early summer when it was rained off, but hooray for the following

Sunday when the match against Newcastle went ahead, providing Mildenhall with a 57-32 win. While all the team scored well it was at reserve that the home team excelled, gaining twenty points to the Newcastle pair's four. Matthew Wright came into the Tigers team for the first time, and was promised more rides after suffering an engine failure and two non-scoring rides. The away meeting at Wolverhampton in the Trophy saw how Mildenhall were a power to be reckoned with when the won well 63-27 and moved to the top of the Trophy mini-league as well as being in a very good position in the League proper table. The junior riders then began their racing in the Southern Junior League with a victory 20-26 over Reading with Thomas Rowlett and Matthew Wright performing well. Mildenhall legend Robert Henry was the young rider's team manager. A defeat at Eastbourne was then turned around at West Row when the Tigers Cubs won 28-8.

For the League KO Cup along came Buxton to Mildenhall for the first leg, and they went home with a ten point lead for their home leg in Derbyshire, when two or three of the Tigers had a distinctly off day; Paul Smith topping the score-chart with a paid twelve. Young Thomas Rowlett suffered a bad fall in heat eight and withdrew from the meeting, as did James Wright of the visitors, for whom Jon Armstrong marked up an eighteen-point maximum. This meeting was run in some rather damp conditions and some riders seemed reluctant to take part. Although Mildenhall turned the tables and won the away leg 47-43 they lost overall by six points. The club were boosted when the firm Superior Exteriors came forward to sponsor the team. They initially thought of advertising in the stadium and the programme, but commercial manager Michael got to work to sign them up as main sponsors.

The headlines in the speedway press and some national newspapers, also involved Mildenhall when they stepped in to sign James Brundle, a young man with a predicted significant future in the sport. He himself spoke of his decision to join Mildenhall and its reputation for helping young riders on their way in the sport. Stand-in captain Paul Lydes-Uing was having a mediocre spell and he himself asked to be left out of the team for a spell to try to build up some confidence once again. The third captain of the Fen Tigers was now appointed in the form of Wayne Broadhurst, who commented "After fifteen years on and off in the sport this is my first post a captain of a team." Wayne's mechanic was former rider with Stoke and Berwick, Glyn Taylor.

Resurrected Wimbledon were next at West Row as the Tigers chalked up another win 60-30, which included eight maximum 5-1 heat wins. After a fall and no points in his first ride Brundle was highest point man with fourteen, and Darren Andrews put in four second places all behind a team member to have a paid maximum; not very often this occurs. The following week-end saw Mildenhall in action for three days on the trot. Friday saw them at Newport, Saturday at Rye House and the return with the Newport Mavericks on Sunday afternoon. On the visit to Hoddesdon, it was clear that with Len Silver taking complete charge the stadium was certainly looking brighter with fresh painting, more building and new changing for the riders. The Fen Tigers were still using 'rider-replacement for the injured Hedge, and were then hit with more as Rowlett suffered concussion, Wright had a hand injury and Thomas Allen had an injured knee. Both away meetings were lost but with eight 5-1 heats and a 5-0, plus providing the winner in thirteen heats, Mildenhall won well against Newport 63-20 in the home meeting and took the bonus point. Gavin Hedge returned to action with three wins. Four Tigers put up maximums, Broadhurst, Hedge, Andrews and Paul Smith. The last heat was not run as the weather took a turn for the worse but the result was allowed to stand.

Riders come and go and Heath Robinson had decided to return to Australia sooner than planned as he was finding it hard to make both ends meet; he had an average of 4.0 from his cluster of rides in England. Two injured riders Paul Smith and Scott James were now back riding and came into the teams reckoning. The home meeting in the Trophy with Swindon saw an uncommon happening when Thomas Allen was in the visiting team instead of the Fen Tigers; this coming about through being in Swindon's Trophy squad.

Halfway through the season and Mildenhall were sitting on top of the league but Peterborough looked the stronger in second place and being two matches in hand; many were saying the champions would be one of these two East Anglian sides, but other teams might have a say in this as some classic encounters were on the cards. Mildenhall's away trip to

Buxton was to run both League and Trophy matches one after the other; this proved a setback for the Fen Tigers when Buxton were the victors in both matches, albeit by a very narrow margin. The temporary signing for Mildenhall of Malcolm Holloway was on the wrong end of a bizarre injury when one of the home riders ran into him after the race had ended, resulting in a dislocated shoulder. Gavin Hedge was still on the sidelines although he had now signed to ride for Stoke in the Premier League as well as the Tigers.

It was an up and down meeting with Kings Lynn, won by Mildenhall 54-36, but Lydes-Uing came back from injury and promptly went back on the side-lines following his first ride in the match. On the other hand, Scott James returned to register a score of paid thirteen, while now at number two Darren Andrews scored fourteen as well as James Brundle (the latter against his former team). Some Conference League teams had begun to take the view that Mildenhall were too strong to take part in this league, but these were answered by the fact that the Tigers had not been winning every match, and even some victories had been on the narrow side. This was most likely down to the fact that team manager Graham Drury always had his ear to the ground and snap up a good rider when he had to, and was not entering a league mean you want to win it. A glance at the league table showed the top five teams were all unbeaten at home while Peterborough were best away from home, losing only two meetings.

A familiar face was in the Carmarthen Dragons side on the visit to Mildenhall in the Trophy, Stuart Williams had been a member of the Tiger Cubs in three of their matches but on signing for the Welsh side had been doing very well for himself and had kept a place in their side with some big scores. A 45-44 Fen Tigers victory threw up the top scorers in Brundle (17+2) and Darren Andrews (13+1) for Mildenhall, and Craig Taylor (13+1) and Matthew Cross (13+3) for the visitors. Graham Drury also spent a lot of time trying to bring Lee Herne to Mildenhall but even though he was eager, the BSPA in their wisdom decided it was not in his the right interests to drop down one league.

Getting through their semi-finals Wayne Broadhurst and James Brundle were the Mildenhall representatives' in the Conference League

Riders Championship on 31 August at Rye House. The Supporters Club presented both Fen Tigers with a new tyre and the cost of their fuel for the Championship Meeting. Unfortunately, both Fen Tigers narrowly missed a place of the rostrum. The eventual winner was Boston's James Birkinshaw with Edward Kennett as runner-up. The meeting everyone was looking forward to (Mildenhall v Peterborough) was something of an anti-climax when it was rained-off, or to be more frank it was 'stormed-off' in fact two very heavy storms one after the other. Malcolm Holloway was to be in the Tigers side for the match as injury threatened to spoil the Mildenhall chances of silverware at the end of the season. This was definitely not helped after the Kings Lynn meeting, which was lost by I single point, plus two more injuries. Thomas Allen fracturing his wrist and was out for the remainder of the season after a high-speed crash into the fence, while Mark Thompson took a nasty blow to his back. both ending up in hospital.

With five teams in the running to be League Champions, and more Mildenhall riders taking spills that saw them injured, Lee Hodgson agreed to sign from Stoke, subject to the BSPA approval. This was given and he appeared in the Trophy meeting versus Wimbledon, won by Mildenhall 60-30 after providing all but one of the heat winners. The transfer deadline of 31 August was also fast approaching as well. Then they hit a poor streak on their travels, and although they were still unbeaten at home, they slipped down the table. Some people pointed to the large turnover in riders as the problem. It as not the case of signing riders all over the place as the Mildenhall Training Schools were being held regularly, master-minded by Michael Lee, Robert Henry and Louis Carr coming along to help. Each time there seemed to be more than ever youngsters coming to these sessions.

Bogy team for the Fen Tigers this year were Buxton but they were also weak travellers, came to visit in the League Trophy, they had surprisingly already beaten Mildenhall in the KO Cup 50-40. Mildenhall paraded a new recruit in 17-year-old Lee Hodgson who had been unhappy at his previous club Stoke, and selected 'rider replacement' for missing Gavin Hedge. Hodgson was doubling up with Workington Comets. The Fen Tigers strong reserve duo Darren Andrews and Scott James were one of the powerful points of the Mildenhall line-up, and so it proved in this fixture when between them they ran up twenty-four of the home sides fifty-five winning points, the young Aussie had already made his trademark with some sweeping moves around the boards at Mildenhall. New man Hodgson weighed in with a double figure score. Ex World Champions Peter Collins, who was with the visiting team, was very complimentary of the track at West Row.

Setting up the track and everything that goes with it is always an extensive operation for each meeting, as the stock cars were very often the night before or coming soon after the speedway meetings. The Mildenhall fence makes use of around one hundred go-cart tyres before the panels of the fence are bolted on. This was before the track could really get the attention for the bikes. Often working into the night a caravan was provided if the staff wished to stay on site, which most of them did, to get things ship=shape in time. These workers are often forgotten but at Mildenhall, they all do their work as strictly volunteers.

The Wolverhampton second string proved no match for the Tigers in the Trophy match, as they lost 67-23, they produced just one heat winner. Mildenhall built on this victory and when the Hitmen came to West Row just two weeks later; the meeting switched to Saturday evening for this one; they repeated their victory and this time for the important league meeting won 56-34., almost a repeat of the Trophy scoreline. With some riders on the way back from nursing injuries, the Fen Tigers helped Wimbledon out as they were struggling to raise a team. Thomas Rowlett and Paul Lydes-Uing were sent out on loan to the London side When some speedway fans suggested that Mildenhall were grabbing all the better riders in the quest for success it was pointed out by Tony Mole that in the main team of Fen Tigers were youngsters with the ages of 17 (2 riders) 16 and 15, underlining Mildenhall's youth policy was still to the fore-front by the promoters.

The Fen Tigers hopes of lifting the Conference League Championship were rather put on hold after a 51-39 loss at Peterborough, who looked very impressive with their all round strength. From the reserve berth, Scott James was the Tigers top scorer with thirteen points. To rub it in Peterborough's Adam Pryer beat James in the Bronze Helmet race. It then remained for Mildenhall to beat both Peterborough and Sheffield at

West Row and for other teams to slip up, and the league could still go to either of three teams. Mildenhall versus Sheffield was yet another meeting, which drew in the crowds as the men from the North were up there in the league table with a chance if any other team faltered. The Tigers however were in top gear at home to the tune of 49-41. With Paul Smith still not quite fit, in came veteran Carl Baldwin to chalk up a score of 9+1 in his helping out role. He remained in the team for the rest of the season, and strictly on merit. With the Fen Tigers also picking up the bonus point they were the only team who had so far grabbed this point against all the other teams.

As a slight distraction and to give the fans a taste of Premier League Speedway, Rye House sent their Premier League side to oppose Mildenhall for a challenge match on 6 October. To bring the Fen Tigers up to a workable strength the Isle of Wight Australian Adam Shields (15+1) the reigning Premier League champion was brought in as a guest as well as Leigh Lanham (15 maximum) plus Reading's Paul Clews. Fen Tigers regulars Scott James, Wayne Broadhurst and Carl Baldwin were included with Jamie Smith a late replacement for Danny Bird. Although Smith fell and pulled out the rest of the meeting Mildenhall gave a good account of themselves as Rye House were victors by only five points, the result being 47-42.

It was the Conference Trophy which gave Mildenhall any chance of silverware and they lay in second place to Carmarthen Dragons, where the Tigers lost before needing a win at Wimbledon and the bonus point to pip the welsh club to the trophy. Wimbledon were having troubles at this time and the Tigers had beaten them three times already this year, so the Tigers and supporters traveled to London in fine voice. 53-37 was the final score of the night to the Fen Tigers who bore the trophy home to West Row. Unfortunately reserve Matt Wright was in hospital after being catapulted into the fence after hitting a fallen rider. The Mildenhall team for this victory was Wayne Broadhurst (11+2), Lee Hodgson (RR), Mark Thompson (6), James Brundle (13), Carl Baldwin (9+1), Darren Andrews (9+3) and Matt Wright (5+1)

With all the results coming in it was all down to the last Mildenhall meeting of the season, when Peterborough Puma's were the visitors on

13 October; and whichever team won they would be champions. Once again, the elements intervened and lots of work was done on the track to try to get this meeting running. As a result, the track was very heavy and the rain started to come down as the racing started. Heat one saw Peterborough put out just one rider - Jason King - which after a restart was a 5-0 to Mildenhall. The visitors put out two in the second heat but went down 5-1, doing slightly better in heat three when the Tigers took a 4-2. It was proving difficult to ride and at this stage Peterborough decided to walk out of the meeting, and Mildenhall took a further three 5-0's before the referee ended the farce and the meeting was abandoned. The times being registered up to this point reflected the conditions, most heat times being ten seconds or more over the track record.

The re-staging of this meeting was fixed for 27 October but damage due to the storms all over East Anglia; this also succumbed to the weather conditions. The Fen Tigers raced their last Trophy meeting at Wimbledon on the 28 October but a lack of other dates saw the Fen Tigers having to travel to Stoke to play off the Peterborough fixture, on the same meeting Newport faced Sheffield to end their season, Stoke being the only track which was able to entertain these matches as most tracks were closed by then. A Mildenhall win would give them the championship but it was not to be and Peterborough took the title instead with their win. The Fen Tigers team for most of the season was composed of Wayne Broadhurst, Gavin Hedge, Mark Thompson, James Brundle, Malcolm Holloway, Darren Andrews, and Scott James.

****

2003
News of the riders came early for Mildenhall. Darren Andrews, Mark Thompson and Thomas Allen had departed for pastures new, and a newcomer to the team was James Mann, who spent the previous three years at Buxton and is hoping for rides with Somerset, and of whom was expected to improve over the next season. However, before a wheel had been turned the injury bug struck. A dislocated shoulder kept Mann out for a few weeks, while Tom Rowlett broke his arm early on. Veteran Carl Baldwin has extended his extensive career and was ready to come into the team at any given time. Another new rider was Kent born Tony Dart who had begun riding in the Youth Development League for Arena Essex in 1998. He had suffered several bad injuries to his legs and had

pins to help them stand up to the rigours of speedway. Ben Howe had also signed; having started his career at seventeen years of age just down the road at Ipswich in 1997 and other clubs included Poole, Kings Lynn, Hull and Newport. From last season, the captain Wayne Broadhirst was again in Fen Tiger colours as was James Brundle, Scott James, Lee Hodgson and Matthew Wright. The Fen Tigers were parading the squad system once again this year, and hoping that the injury season that was 2002 will not be repeated.

The management had applied for and been successful in selected as the track to stage the Four-Team Tournament for the Conference League, plus the British Under 21 Qualifying Round towards the end of March. One more change was to the race-day, and it was back to the traditional Mildenhall day of Sunday.

As for the League there were thirteen teams competing, and in the Trophy nine teams; some being in the Trophy only which saw newcomers in Armadale, Iwade and Trelawny. In all seventeen teams being involved in various Conference League fixtures, the largest ever. The league was proving a stepping stone for young riders coming into the sport and older riders who want to just continue in the sport for the love of it.

Mildenhall made a very early start; on 15 March they swung into action with a Conference Trophy match against Wimbledon, who were in the charge of Dingle Brown for so long the master at Mildenhall, helping them through the early days of 1990's when the re-surfaced from their enforced break. The Fen Tigers came out on top 48-42 in a highly competitive meeting. Scott James top scored with a well deserved 13+1.

The following week they hosted the first-leg of a Three-team Tournament, and coasted to victory with 52 against Boston (29) and Peterborough (26). The Boston leg also saw Mildenhall top with 42, Boston Barracuda Braves (36) & Peterborough Puma's (29). The third leg at Peterborough was on 5 April and Mildenhall finished top dogs on 136, well ahead of the other teams.

Then came the first prestige meeting of the year, the British Under 21 Championship Qualifier at Mildenhall. Twenty-four of the best young riders were on show in what at first seemed a very complicated system that took a bit of time for the programme fans to work out with calculators' in one hand and pens in the other. Eight riders were seeded through to meet eight more who battled their way to the later stages. It was a star-studded field of young hopeful's which included the likes of Barry Evans, James Cockle, and Richie Hawkins together with Fen Tigers representatives James Brundle, James Mann and Lee Hodgson. However, winner turned out to be Jason King with Ben Wilson in second place and Daniel King in third. Chris Mills was fourth. The League officials who were on hand congratulated the Mildenhall promoters and staff on a job well done. Fen Tiger Hodgson reached the Under 21 Final by way of the Qualifier at Sheffield.

Starting their away meetings in the League the Fen Tigers were worth their 47-43 victory at Newport where Wayne Broadhurst kept a hold on the Bronze Helmet, although his challenger from Newport could not ride in the race for the honour; having problems with his machinery. In the Conference Trophy Mildenhall easily beat Buxton 59-31 with Scott James thundering to a paid maximum (14+1), as Buxton paraded four new riders in their team. James was set to ride for Coventry when not riding for the Fen Tigers, and the young Australian came up against some fellow riders from down under, whom he had already beaten in his home country.

The result of Carmarthen 41 Mildenhall 50 saw the second away win so far, but the Tigers were quickly brought back to earth the next evening at Rye House. Their long time rivals inflicting the first defeat of the season on Mildenhall by the margin of eleven points, 51-40. Only a week before a speedway reporter described the Fen Tigers as awesome, but as they say, pride comes before a fall, so it was to be seen how Mildenhall cope with this loss. They went out and signed sixteen-year-old Daniel King who wanted away from Peterborough and Ipswich grabbed him and just as quickly loaned him to Mildenhall, which was where the young man wanted to be. At Rye House Carl Baldwin, who had been going great guns, was involved in a crash resulting in broken ribs and will be off for some time. Then Lee Hodgson suffered concussion when riding for Somerset and too will be on the side for a short while. After defending the bronze helmet successfully in Wales Broadhurst lost it at Rye House to Edward Kennett.

Expecting an exciting season ahead the 'King of Travel' Perry was busy arranging coaches for all of the away meetings. He promised reclining seats, drinks and videos to watch and while the time away. Buxton, Stoke and Newcastle were filling up very quickly, and if these trips are as good as previous years, the supporters were in for a wonderful time. News of former Fen Tigers found Darren Andrews now at Oxford and Thomas Allen with Swindon.

Boston were the successful visitors to West Row the next week, and after their good start the Fen Tigers had now lost two matches on the run, " had the bubble burst ?" those in the know were asking. The victorious Boston had a line-up filled with ex Fen Tigers, Mark Thompson, Dean Garrod, Peter Boast and Rob Hollingworth. Mildenhall 44 Boston 46 being the final score in an action packed Trophy match, in which the injuries to James Mann and Daniel King no doubt played a major part in the result. The experiment on 4 May by getting in two meetings (Buxton and Stoke) on the same day did not work as the trip to Derbyshire was called off, a victim of the elements, but the Stoke meeting was on with Mildenhall running the home team quite ragged, as they were all out to avenge their two losses. The Fen Tigers winning 53-36. It was also the Carmarthen Dragons who also felt the backlash as the Fen Tigers returned to their home meetings with a 66-23 win over their visitors from Wales. Every Mildenhall rider was paid for a double figure score except one who could only reach nine points. Ben Howe came into the team in place of Mann whose injury look set to keep him off a bike for a while. Young Tom Rowlett, who was in the Tigers team at Stoke, found himself an honorary Dragon when the visitors arrived a rider short. The operation of the squad system meant even the captain had to take a turn of having a rest but Wayne Broadhurst and wife still turned up at West Row to watch and encourage the others in the Mildenhall team. It was an anti-climax when the fixture at Wolverhampton was rained off. This was quickly followed by another postponement when the KO Cup meeting at Oxford also fell to the weather.

With both sides looking to have a big season the Mildenhall versus Peterborough clash attracted a large following at West Row; it also sported the two King brothers but now in different teams. The final score was 56-33 in favour of the home team with James, Howe and Daniel King in double figures, while Peterborough suffered two injuries. The Tigers then followed this with a home victory over Buxton, James Brundle putting together an excellent fifteen point maximum. This was in a meeting that suffered a rainstorm at the halfway point, but patience was rewarded when the track staff got to work and made the strip fit for racing once again for the meeting to be run to the finish. Next evening in unpleasant weather, the Hitmen had their revenge when they won 47-43 in Derbyshire. Some Fen Tigers were getting more rides in the Premier League and the time came when fixtures began to clash so out went manager Drury and signed Lee Howard who was with Stoke in the Trophy meetings; this was further cover for injured or unavailable riders. Howard was only to ride in League and Cup matches. The team manager was absent when he was called in for TV to be a judge of Scrapheap Challenge; this was when contestants had to make a motorbike out of bits and pieces of scrap metal.

A very high-energy tussle at West Row, the Fen Tigers put one over another of their close rival Rye House by 48-44, with the visitors Edward Kennett in great form and well worth his nineteen points. The home supporters saw how their Tigers could fight for a victory when early on Sunday it was not known what the team was to be. Daniel King had injured himself the night before at Kings Lynn, James Brundle crashed in the same meeting while food poisoning seemed to have downed Ben Howe. Add to this the fact that skipper Broadhurst was riding with broken ribs it was a wonder a side could be put together. However, the squad system saved the day. Lee Hodgson was diverted to West Row as he was heading elsewhere and Brundle rode despite his pain, and Scott James was due a rest but he had to ride as his mother was over from Australia to see him in action. One Tigers rider Thomas Rowlett asked for a transfer and he joined up with Peterborough where he had the chance for more rides than he was getting at Mildenhall.

Mildenhall seemed to have no trouble in building up a substantial sixteen point lead versus Oxford in the first leg of the KO Cup Round,

Ricky Scarboro making an appearance for the visitors as their captain with ex Tiger Darren Andrews also in the Oxford line-up. Rowlett was a late inclusion for Oxford while the Fen Tigers elected to put only one rider out in three heats, as James Brundle was a non-starter. Mildenhall were now on a winning streak and accounted for Wimbledon, Swindon, Wolverhampton and Newport in quick succession. Team manager Drury was kept on his toes with several injuries and thought at one stage he was to ask anyone who could ride a motor-cycle to have a ride. It was to his credit he had many connections in the speedway world that riders seemed to be plucked out of the air when specially needed; well done Graham! One such rider Lee Howard (Newcastle) jumped at the chance to help in one meeting but rang up in the morning to say his van had given up the ghost and he could not make the journey to West Row.

It was always quite difficult to get speedway talked about more in the national newspapers but Mildenhall's Tony Dart did just that when a large spread in the Sun newspaper, revealing his determination to ride on after suffering several near career ending injuries. All this also reflected back to his club the Fen Tigers. How he has progressed in the sport was seen when he had a guest outing with Kings Lynn.

The league table at this time placed Rye House on top and the Fen Tigers second, both with eighteen points but with Mildenhall having had a match less. Boston were the ones to watch as they had only been beaten once so far and the Tigers had to pay them a visit very soon. The Trophy table had Mildenhall on top as they were defending the silverware they won the previous year. The looked for conflict of the Tigers and the Barracudas did not take place as the now familiar rain clouds opened up again on the Boston rage night.

Mildenhall added to their list of victories with Newcastle, Oxford and Trelawny falling to the Fen Tigers. These came with another injury, this time it was the Australian flyer Scott James, who was to be out for longer than at first thought. Straightaway into the Mildenhall fold came Nick Simmons who had been looking for a change of scenery after trying his luck in the Premier League. He made his debut at Trelawny and scored fourteen points.

The prestige meeting of the season then took centre stage at West Row, the Conference League Four-Team Championship. However, the heavens (again!) opened with a thunderstorm during the meeting, and was provisionally re-dated for 5 October, again at West Row. The semi-finals had been completed leaving the four teams in the final, but it was not sure for some weeks whether the whole meeting would be run again or a meeting with the four finalists only. These were Boston, Peterborough, Mildenhall and Rye House.

Back in the Fen Tigers camp there was a bit of an injury crisis and never one to cancel meetings manager Drury travelled to Armadale with just one heat leader (Broadhurst) and two reserves Dart and Wright. John Branney, Karl Langley and Keith Maben were taken into the side when the Tigers arrived in Scotland, but this could not help them and they suffered their biggest defeat of the season 61-32. On to Buxton the next day and although losing again they managed to take the bonus point as Ricky Scarboro and Benji Compton were drafted in as guests to play their part for the Tigers, together with Andrew Jackson. After this dire trip to the north, Benji Compton and Danny Norton were taken on board the Tigers bus, but the other news was that Danny King and Le Hodgson were taking a break from Conference League matches as they were now having regular meetings in the Premier League.

Losing by just one point at Oxford in the KO Cup the Fen Tigers went through to the semi-finals due to their home victory. Newcomers Trelawny were next at West Row and found the Tigers determined to gain the points, Danny Norton coming into the team in place of Tony Dart and Tom Rowlett at number four, and with James Brundle back again they won 52-38. High fliers Sheffield were expected to give Mildenhall a run for their money and certainly test the home record of the Fen Tigers, who had Tony Dart absent after a sickening crash at Oxford where he was sent over the safety fence on to the greyhound track; Nick Lee taking his place. As it happened, the score-line of 63-26 to the Tigers was not the close match everyone thought. Sheffield top scorers were Luke Priest and Richard Hall with nine apiece and their reserve pairing contributed just one point between them. Mildenhall's riders took all but one heat victories to sweep aside their visitors. Next evening the trip to Sheffield for the return fixture produced a draw, both teams scoring forty-five points, Mildenhall gaining the bonus point. This could well have been a Fen Tigers win as James Brundle blew an engine within sight of the finish when well placed in the last heat.

Yet another fresh rider was brought to West Row in the face of Paul Lee, who had been sitting out the present season but was eager to get back into the saddle. He had spent 2002 at Swindon and had ridden for Coventry and Sheffield in his career so far. The away meeting at Wimbledon produced an interesting statistic when Ben Howe amassed a total of 23 including a golden double; but didn't prevent Tigers losing 48-45 in the Trophy

The top meetings were coming thick and fast and a team looking to be champions were Boston who met Mildenhall at West Row on 17 August. Once again the Tigers showed their teeth and took the honours at 50-39. James Brundle also snatched the Bronze Helmet away from Trevor Harding. Dart attempted a comeback after his injury but withdrew after two rides. Boston's Aussie Trevor Harding led his team well in a meeting which saw four Mildenhall riders suffering a blown engine; very expensive. Everybody was hoping these did not affect their push for honours.

Showing the team spirit at Mildenhall, young Matt Wright was busy in the pits cleaning the skipper, Broadhurst, bike during the meetings while his family were ferrying Wayne around the tracks while his own transport was off the road. Wright himself was enjoying many more outings this current season. All pulling together was then to the fore when the Tigers travelled to Carmarthen when Brundle had transport problems and Hodgson was marooned in Bank Holiday traffic jam on the way; both never made it to Wales. Nick Simmons and Danny Norton set to and upped their game and both registered paid maximums (eighteen points each) to give Mildenhall a remarkable win. The team had been made up with Russell Barnett a local junior. To help cover the reserve berths Brendan was then added to the Mildenhall squad. One of the best performances of the season so far was going to Swindon and tasting victory 48-42 to keep the Tigers ahead of the rest in the league table.

After sitting on top of the league for several weeks the Fen Tigers slipped up in two away meetings, Wimbledon in the Trophy and then in the league at Wolverhampton. The home meeting with Wimbledon introduced Paul Lee to the Tigers line-up, and he did not disappoint when top scoring with thirteen. After a rather hectic August, the Fen Tigers filled in an open Sunday with a Handicapped Best Pair Meeting. This saw Brendan MacKay at West Row as a Fen Tiger. Luke Priest, Darren Smith and a young Lee Smart were also in the field, which saw a return to the saddle of a past favourite in Robert Henry who had Carl Baldwin as his partner, and although they did not set the track alight, they delighted fans with some spirited riding. Paul Lee and Tony Dart were top of the pile.

With the scramble to fit in the fixtures Mildenhall put on a 'double-header' at West Row on 13 September. The first match was against Carmarthen Dragons whom Mildenhall won comfortably by 68-22 as five Tigers put up double figure scores. The second of the two matches was more important being the first leg of the League K O Cup versus old rivals Boston Barracuda Braves. Although the Mildenhall line-up was the same as the first match, changes were made in the positions to give them a more solid look, and they went out to put twenty points between the Fen Tigers and Boston, so setting up a good second leg. A draw at Boston confirmed that Mildenhall had reached the final, a fact that put a smile on many a Fen Tigers supporter.

Unfortunately, this feeling of contentment was quickly dimmed when Swindon registered a protest that Mildenhall had included an illegal rider at their home meeting two weeks previously. Team manager Graham Drury had sent the list of the riders to Swindon well before the meeting and nothing had been said until several days after it had taken place. Although Mildenhall said they had done no wrong the powers that were decided that Lee Hodgson's average was too high for him to ride at Reserve, so his seven points were deducted, with the result then changed from a Tigers win to a loss by one point 42-41. This meant the Mildenhall effort to be champions was proving slightly harder. The League and its officials were by now joining the cause in line with some other sports and after the Peterborough meeting Brundle and James Horton were selected for a random dope test; which showed negative.

After six years the track record was broken by Paul Lee in the third heat of the meeting versus Newcastle Gems; the new time being 51.37. The match produced another win victory for Mildenhall 67-23. As the Tigers produced the winner in fourteen of the fifteen heats, and five Mildenhall riders were in double figures, and there were eleven 5-1 heat wins. It seemed it was going to be Mildenhall's year. Indeed one of the biggest wins the Tigers had ever had over near rivals Peterborough was at Kings Lynn in the second of a double-hearer, which ended 65-25 to Mildenhall. (Matt Wright 12+3, Paul Lee 12, James Brundle 12). There was much comment at the time about the teams Peterborough were fielding, amid indifferent conversations.

The Tigers leap-frogged over Rye House to the top again, and then Boston jumped to the top over Tigers by winning at Carmarthen. Then Paul Lee netted a maximum (12) as Mildenhall ousted Boston from the top of Trophy league by winning 52-38 over Stoke Spitfires.

At last the re-run Conference League 4-Team Championships were staged at West Row, with just four teams involved. Opposing Mildenhall were Rye House, Boston and Peterborough. Despite putting up twenty-nine points the Fen Tigers had to give best to Rye House who managed one point more to win the meeting. Mildenhall provided six heat winners and Rye House five, but the Tigers lost James Brundle with a broken wrist after two rides although Matt Wright scored five points from his two reserve rides. With two heats to go Mildenhall were three points in front and had only to score points in the final two heats, but then had two falls, which handed the trophy to Rye House. There were several ex Fen Tigers on view that night; Daniel King and Danny Norton for Peterborough, Barry Evans for Rye House and Mark Thompson and Peter Boast in the Boston colours. Brundle joined James Mann and Scott James on the injured list for the remainder of the season. There were also some rumblings amongst all the teams at some referee's decisions and Len Silver the Rye House team manager earned himself a fine for protesting too much, but he was only doing what nearly all the managers were thinking.

Despite immense efforts, Boston could not stop Mildenhall collecting vital 46-44 win at Saddlebow Rd, and two days later big efforts from

-81-

Tony Dart (12+3) James Brundle (12) Wayne Broadhurst (11+1) saw the Fen Tigers romp to a win to extend their lead at top, crushing Newcastle 67-23. There was no doubt that Paul Lee was going great in Mildenhall's stride to the top, although some other promotions were hinting that he should be doing all this in his own(!) Premier League. However, Graham Drury had seized the opportunity when Lee was looking for a way back into the sport. On 9 October Paul Lee showed a clean pair of heels in winning the Oz Chem Top Gun Championship at Sheffield, and proceeded to strike another max as Mildenhall defeated Armadale 50-40 in a Trophy match at West Row.

With so many ifs and buts over the final few meetings of the season it all came down to Rye House losing at Sheffield to at last see Mildenhall champions of the Conference League once again since 1979, two points clear of Rye House and Oxford a further six points adrift. When Tony Mole had taken over the club at the beginning of 2002, he was not afraid to put money into the venture and it paid off with some silverware, and put the name of Mildenhall Fen Tigers squarely on the British Speedway map.

The season was far from finished however as the first and second in the league in 2003 met each other in the KO Cup Final, the first leg being at Hoddesdon, where the two arch-rivals were always within three points of each other. Daniel King, to everybody's surprise in at Reserve, and Paul Lee put in sparkling performances to help keep the scores down to a slender lead of three points for Rye House. Many an eyebrow was raised within the ranks of the teams in the Conference League at the younger brother King in the Fen Tigers team, especially so in a reserve berth, allowing for his near nine average in the Premier league, but nobody officially done anything more than smile at Mr Drury's standpoint. The only blot at the time was that Tony Dart was left out of the team at Hoddesdon as a disciplinary measure, Benji Compton having his second meeting with Mildenhall in the first leg. The second leg at West Row started badly when Wayne Broadhurst injured his hand in winning the opening heat, and took no further part for the rest of the afternoon. With the score always close heat eleven saw Lee and visiting James Cockle collide in the back straight, and the Mildenhall rider got up to win the re-run although in some pain. It came down to the Tigers wanting a maximum heat win and Paul Lee, who learned he had broken his jaw, mounted on a borrowed bike, onto which he had to be helped, clinched the victory 91-87 overall) in a never-to-be-forgotten ride to bring the cup to West Row, with the supporters dancing in the stands. The two reserves had also taken the meeting by the scruff of the neck with Tony Dart (12+2) and Daniel King - back in the fold - (12+3) helping to guide the team to victory.

There was the matter also of the Trophy and its destination, in which the Fen Tigers had to travel to Kings Lynn to meet Boston in the last match, which was in fact the decider, as whoever won would take the Trophy. On the night, the Boston Barracuda Braves gave an excellent display to beat Mildenhall 50-40. To be fair the Fen Tigers were missing Broadhurst, Brundle, Hodgson and Howe as well as long term injured Mann and James, although Lee wound up his comeback season with eighteen points from seven rides. Danny Norton, Nick Simmonds and Benji Compton were also in the Mildenhall line-up. With Dart and Simmons spearheading the Tigers team - both in double figures - the Fen Tigers ended their magnificent season by losing at Oxford 53-37, giving Oxford third place in the league table. Just three Mildenhall riders were in the last team as they picked up three juniors on the night, Rhys Wilding, Lawrence Needs and Jason Newitt.

With many different starting times for home meetings over the season, one of the last programmes for the season contained a questionnaire for supporters to have their say in what time would suit everyone. Next season it was agreed not to issue season tickets to fans, the reason being that there was a very poor response to this idea in the current season. Looking at the statistics for the season Mildenhall used twenty-eight different riders along the way, a very high number by a team that was victorious in League and KO Cup. It must be said however that many of these just rode one meeting and in some cases only one ride, when Mildenhall were short of riders for away meetings but fulfilled their obligations although down on rider numbers. As early as the second Conference League match the Fen Tigers had to include Matt Tutton when they visited his home track Newport. The same happened at Newcastle when local lad Scott Nettleship found himself in the Mildenhall line-up, and Lee Howard was a Fen Tiger for their

-83-

meeting at Wolverhampton.

****

2004

Graham Drury set to and built another Fen Tigers team that was hoped to challenge for league honours again for 2004, but one rider he had to replace was the 2003 captain Wayne Broadhurst who had left West Row to settle at Wimbledon. A clause hardly ever used was put in place by the Mildenhall chief on his former rider having to serve a twenty-eight day ban on riding for his new club, it was alleged that Wimbledon had approached the rider and poached him in the close season. After riding at reserve in the knock-out cup final Danny King was back with the Tigers and joined by his brother Jason King, their Premier League side Arena Essex moving up to the Elite League. They were joined by Paul Lee the former Long Eaton and Sheffield asset, who had switched to the Fen Tigers during the previous season. Highly promising James Brundle was also sporting the Mildenhall colours once again as was long serving rider Carl Baldwin. Ex Stoke Nick Simmons returned to West Row and two other riders added to the strong line-up were Richie Hawkins from Swindon and Chris Collins from Buxton. Two more astute signings making up the squad were the reserve pair of Lee Smart and Darren Smith. Lee Hodgson, who had not re-signed for the Fen Tigers, made a comeback for Stoke in mid-season, and Mark Thompson was with Weymouth.

As for the make-up of the Conference League for 2004, two teams had departed namely Wolverhampton 'Wolf Cubs' and Trelawney 'Pitbulls'. There were however an influx of new teams, Weymouth 'Wildcats', Coventry 'Cougars', Armadale, Stoke, Kings Lynn 'Starlets' and Sittingbourne 'Crusaders'. On the brand new tracks front Norwich had a request to join the league turned down in the January of 2004 when Kings Lynn objected as they were too near to their home in Saddlebow Road. The newborn Plymouth 'Devils' were also turned down, even after being given the go ahead by the BSPA; strange decision this! However, Scunthorpe 'Scorpions' were allowed to run some challenge matches during the season. There were some teams competing in the League only and the same for the Trophy meetings; Peterborough and Sheffield being two of these in the latter only; Sittingbourne were to ride in the KO Cup only. A new experiment at the request of the SCB was implemented at Mildenhall when the 'first aiders' were not on the centre-green but stationed in the crowd.

This year a major change in the rules needed clarifying the 'Tactical Ride' and the 'Tactical Substitute'. The former ride is permitted when the team goes down to eight points behind and must be the rider nominated for that heat, and only two tactical rides were allowed each team. As for the 'Tactical Substitute' is also only allowed when a team goes eight points in arrears but starting fifteen metres handicap on gate four; this rider could be replacing another programmed rider. Scores for both the substitute and ride were doubled but they must finish in front of an opposing rider. These rules seemed to be changed quite a bit over the seasons and still cause some scratched heads in the pits on occasions. Some experts soon pointed out that a team could purposely not win a heat to stay just out of reach of a 'tactical ride or substitute, but there were many supporters who said not many team managers would stoop so low, and everyone would abide by the book, but?

It was a dreadful start to the season as riders and fans made two trips to Boston, only to see the meeting called off through the rain. This was to be a challenge match before the serious matters started. After rain during the day, the heavy rain just before the start meant no racing after both captains and referee Mick Bates had inspected the track and agreed it was not safe. The home match of this challenge actually began and the first heat was run, but seeing horrible conditions and the steady rain, the meeting had to be abandoned. Some speedway followers brought up the old question of cover for the tracks in bad weather, and the expense would certainly be worth it to get the meetings going along regularly in spite of the early season poor weather.

Fingers were crossed when the visitors to West Row, which was now the opening meeting, were Newcastle Gems. This match went ahead as the new track manager, the infamous 'Huggy' was now back in the fold, and being described as the best in the business, having been in with Mildenhall right from the early days of straw bales as the safety fence. In the past, some supporters had been parking their cars in the rider's car park and walking through the pits to their place on the terraces, but Health and Safety stepped in to put a ban on this practice. Talk of starting the season even earlier had been rapidly talked down when the weather turned out to be well against this. Mildenhall duly won the first meeting 54-38 with new reserve Lee Smart notching top points of twelve plus one. One incident, which did not very often occur, was when Jason King's bike suddenly caught fire when on the starting line, a quick response by starting marshal Graham Thompson however soon put this out; quick thinking or what?

One of the early meetings was the Mildenhall visit to Plough Lane to face the Wimbledon Dons, who paraded in their side three former Fen Tigers Barrie Evans, Matthew Wright and Gavin Hedge. Mildenhall took the points in a close 48-45 match. Making a comeback after a bad injury to his wrists, Gavin had been captain of the Fen Tigers for two seasons. The Plough Lane meeting was a poor one for the London side and the fans were left wondering what had got into Wimbledon, with only two of their riders showing some urgency. The Fen Tigers were also well motivated by the programme notes in the Wimbledon programme, which were definitely not humble in their view of the Mildenhall team and there way of bringing a squad of riders together rather than just a seven man team.

The second meeting at West Row was the prestigious British Under 21 Championship semi-final with the cream of young talent fighting for a place in the final. Daniel King, Lee Smart and James Brundle were the Fen Tigers on display and all three getting through. This made it five Fen Tigers in the final, Richie Hawkins and Jason King were seeded straight in to the final; people were asking was this a record, but it certainly highlighted what Mildenhall were about with their young talent. For Lee Smart it was a fine performance as he was only fifteen years of age when he qualified. There was a bigger than usual crowd for the semi-final at West Row on 4 April, and the size of the crowd drew the comment for Graham Drury the if this was always the case it would help the cause of Mildenhall seeking to join the Premier League.

There was some last moment switching around when the challenge match against Rye House was made into a League fixture. The scoreline of 53-40 showed how strong the Fen Tigers were although the Rye House team looked due for another year near to the top of the league. Rivals for many years the referee had to venture out of his box to come into the pits and speak to the riders and managers of both teams, telling them to calm it down just a little; Rye House team manager had incurred a fine for some comments and/or actions.

The great start to the season for James Brundle was not unnoticed by the Premier League teams and he was now riding regularly at Kings Lynn, so an agreement between the two clubs saw his many rides were regulated so as not see the young rider 'burn out'. Just at that time, he had ridden five days in a row so a break in his matches for Mildenhall was called for. One of last seasons success stories was Tony Dart who had surprisingly not found a place in a Conference team, and he was brought back into the Tigers lair.

The KO Cup first leg versus Carmarthen was won 52-31, although this does not tell all. The threatening rain began in earnest just before heat fourteen, and the way it poured down there was no way the remaining heats could be run so the match was stopped and the score stood. The main talking point before the next meeting was that Chris Collins had decided to retire and concentrate on his business interests. This was a shame as he had shown some fine form in the early meetings. To help compensate for this young Adam Roynon was brought down south from Newcastle to West Row. He had been offered to Wimbledon who decided he was not quite good enough! Signing Roynon meant that Darren Smith had to be left out of the line-up to comply with the rules.

The expected hard match with Wimbledon did not turn out so when the Tigers logged up a 59-33 victory, the visiting team did not really perform at all well on the day. Regarding old and young teams the average age for the Fen Tigers in this meeting was eighteen and the Wimbledon team was thirty. Danny King was being used by Graham Drury in a reserve berth for Mildenhall, although he was with (and riding for) Ipswich, but at a hearing two months into the season he was told he was not eligible to ride in the Conference League, couldn't and did not ride for the Fen Tigers in the remainder of the season. The highlight of the next weekend was seeing Richie Hawkins crowned British Under 21 Champions after the final at Rye House. This was the first time that a rider representing Mildenhall had won this prestigious

-87-

(11 top) MILDENHALL 2005 LINE-UP
(11 bottom) MARK THOMPSON

(12 top) BARRY EVANS
(12 bottom) versus old rivals RYE HOUSE

**(13 top) MILDENHALL'S 1st PREMIER LEAGUE TEAM
(13 bottom) JON ARMSTRONG**

(14) JASON LYONS

(15 top) 2007 MILDENHAL FEN TIGERS
(15 bottom) KYLE LEGAULT

(16 right) JAN GRAVESEN

(16 left) JARI MAKINEN

event, and he proudly showed off his trophy before the Weymouth meeting. The King brothers also scored enough to go through to the European meeting at Latvia. Jason did not progress any further by Daniel went through to the World semi-final.

Captain Paul Lee who had returned to the sport during the previous season, and nailed his colours to the West Row mast headed the Mildenhall team. He was sharing the role of captain with veteran Carl Baldwin who was on standby whenever he was needed, and not a regular competitor, although he did decide to hang up his leathers for good a little way into the season, but was to be a coach for the youngsters coming through the Mildenhall factory. For the second leg of the KO Cup at Carmarthen, James Brundle, who had come along to support the team, decided to ride instead of Mildenhall using rider-replacement. He borrowed Tony Darts's spare leathers and put together a bike of bits and pieces from here and there. With the Fen Tigers reserve riders going nicely it meant that young Rhys Wilding, another track school rider on the Tigers books, was getting only limited rides, and after asking for a transfer joined Oxford.

Richie Hawkins success story of the season so far meant Berwick soon snapped him up, although he will still ride for Mildenhall when available. Attempts top bring in two more riders to Mildenhall who had no team at the time, was also blocked by the BSPA, stating it made the Fen Tigers too strong. This attitude was beginning to frustrate the promoters, as they were due to be short of riders especially the King brothers for two meetings as they travel abroad in the Under 21 Championships. The meeting with Swindon saw the return of Darren Smith together with Jon Armstrong and Buxton provided the opposition for the first Bank Holiday meeting for the Fen Tigers at West Row. Riding in his first match for Mildenhall was young fifteen-year-old Scott Campus, who at number eight in a rider-replacement team, was given four rides. In the 59-35 victory Armstrong registered his first paid maximum, and a paid twelve from Lee; both outscored by Lee Smart with sixteen plus two from his six rides.

Jason King then had to sit out a few meetings when an old back injury flared up once again, and this cost him a place in the Conference League

Best Pairs Championship at Wimbledon. Jon Armstrong partnered Richie Hawkins for this event. For the first time for many years the trip north yielded two wins, at Armadale and Newcastle, indeed a fine week-end all round as the many supporters who travelled by coach or cars made the two meetings sound like home meetings for the riders and management. In the victory at Weymouth Paul Lee broke their track record and back at West Row done the same in the Swindon match. Six weeks on the sidelines was the fate of Adam Roynon after a bad spill in the Buxton meeting, which resulted in a broken right wrist; just when he was sitting his school exams as well! Luckily, Tony Dart was back in the reckoning after serving a two-match ban by the club for missing the Northern Tour.

Mildenhall however continued to march on and by the beginning of June they had stretched their unbeaten start to the season to fifteen matches, and stood on top of the Conference League and already talk was of retaining the championship for a second year. They were on fire, and Lee Smart took that literally in the meeting at Newcastle when his bike suddenly caught fire when he was having a practice start; it was soon snuffed out however after giving him quite a fright. Pride comes before a fall however and the Fen Tigers went out and promptly lost their unbeaten record, and at home as well. The worst thing of all was that it was long-term rivals the Barracuda Braves from Boston who were the winners, but by only two points. 47-45. A 5-1 in the last heat would have given Mildenhall a draw but they only chalked up a 4-2 when their top man Richard Hall split the Fen Tigers pair of Armstrong and Lee. These two Tigers were in double figures but the rest of the team were strictly off colour.

Mildenhall, in spite of this, came back and gained two away wins at Swindon and Carmarthen, two tracks where the home teams usually reign supreme. It was at the track in Wales that a problem came up when Paul Lee did not turn up and incurred a fine from the referee of £50. He had been signed for Kings Lynn but everyone thought he would have his last meeting for the Fen Tigers and the promoters were disappointed; in his place of captain was Richie Hawkins and Mildenhall duly won at Carmarthen by 46-42, although Hawkins did not ride as he was on duty with his Premier League Berwick. Back in the team Darren Smith was struggling and a hypnotist was engaged to help him as it was thought it was all in his head, thinking of a bad crash he had at Sheffield some years previously. Jason King was returning after injury and proved he had not lost his skill with a four-ride maximum versus Newport Mavericks in a heavy win 66-26. In the team for the first time was yet another youngster Kyle Hughes who hailed from Swindon and already knew Lee Smart and Gary Phelps another signing from his part of the world.

As the League KO Cup holders the Fen Tigers had to face neighbours Kings Lynn Starlets in the Second Round, and were at home for the first leg at the end of June. The Lynn youngsters had come into the Conference League at the last minute when the Puma's of Peterborough withdrew. Hoping the rain would hold off the meeting got underway but by the time of heat eleven, the rain decided to come down, and with the Tigers leading 43-17, the meeting had to be abandoned. Then followed a trip to Coventry in the trophy when Mildenhall extended their unbeaten run in the Trophy. Nevertheless, the victory came at a cost when Lee Smart tumbled down the track after a bad crash that meant a trip to hospital where he had a much damaged finger sorted out as well as several bumps and bruises. Smart had been included in the Great Britain Under 21 team to tour Sweden in August, Mildenhall's Hawkins was also selected as the captain of the squad, and had celebrated his post with breaking the track record at Coventry.

Kyle Hughes was another Fen Tigers noted as he was in the Under fifteen Championship at Buxton. Still encouraging younger riders Mildenhall gave an outing to Danny Betson a sixteen-year-old, in the home meeting with Stoke Spitfires, which also saw Kevin Long take over as Announcer and Presenter from Mike Boswell who had been in that position for many years at West Row. England's top rider Scott Nicholls paid a visit to West Row for this meeting and was soon surrounded for autographs and photographs.

Mildenhall took their first silverware of the season when they were crowned Four-Team Champions at Stoke. The Fen Tigers were Jason King, Jon Armstrong, Gary Phelps and Tony Dart with Lee Smart an un-used reserve. To be fair the riders struggled a bit in the semi-finals finishing runners-up in their hard looking group, but in the final it was a different story as they got it together and cheered on by the coach load of supporters they proved the winners. The following day Wimbledon visited West Row in the Trophy and the only thing that went on the blink was the public address system which was proving a bit temperamental but work was in progress to fix the faults; Wimbledon were beaten 52-43.

Just when things were seemingly going along well, it was learned that Jason King was joining Rye House as a short-term replacement for their injured Steve Masters. It was a step up for him as he had been putting in some first-class performances for the Tigers of late. While disappointing in some ways it was a credit to Mildenhall that they had helped talented riders of the Paul Lee and Richie Hawkins type as well as Jason, to up their career. To cover for the loss James Mann was brought into the Tigers line-up, having been on the sidelines for a while with shoulder injuries that needed surgery, but had been getting rid of the rusty parts which not riding does. Armadate Devils were the next and took the Tigers to a last heat decider before losing 47-46 to a Mildenhall team who lost Hughes in the second heat for the rest of the meeting. The Scottish team also lost their Aussie captain Matthew Wethers and the crowd were treated to the sight of the air ambulance helicopter touching down on the centre green to whisk him off to hospital. The following week a collection was made in aid of the Air Ambulance, which saw them presented with £286-02.

After a car accident, James Brundle was back in the saddle after just eight weeks for the match against Kings Lynn Starlets in the KO Cup, won by Mildenhall 63-27. Richie Hawkins had been in Sweden riding for his country, and as captain, in two meetings. After the Australian Under 21 side could not fulfil their match at West Row against the Great Britain Under 21's the Fen Tigers took on the Great Britain side, with James and Lee Smart switching to the GB line-up for this event. Danny King was included in the GB team as well but the BSPA put their oar in again and refused to let him ride on a Conference League track! The Fen Tigers welcomed back Jason King from his loan spell at Rye House. Although the Fen Tigers lost 49-43 the meeting was a grand advert for Conference League riders.

By the end of August Mildenhall were sitting on top of the League and the Trophy table, and there was no doubt that they were one of the most entertaining and successful teams. The only down side was the strange fact that the attendance figures had dipped slightly in the previous few weeks. The better news was that the Fen Tigers were through to the semi-finals of the KO Cup when, after some strange happening from just up the A10, the Kings Lynn side were excluded from the second-leg versus Mildenhall. The long period of inclement bad weather saw several meetings called off but the Tigers were lucky, more so when they looked at the numerous meetings to be fixed in, and some double-headers looked on the cards.

The Welsh Bank Holiday week=end saw both Carmarthen and Newport beaten. Gary Phelps was out for the rest of the season after a spill at Newport, he had broken his elbow and his thumb. The last heat was not re-run as it was gathering dusk and no medical cover was available, so both managers agreed to end the proceedings then with the score counting. It was a strange looking Tigers side that opposed Carmarthen with four riders missing and two rookies making their debut, but Jon Armstrong, Tony Dart and Lee Smart putting up eleven heat wins between them. Rob Smith and trainee Daniel Blake were the two youngsters to make their first appearance for Mildenhall.

A double-header saw the Fen Tigers take on Oxford in the KO Cup (first leg) and then a Trophy match versus Kings Lynn, both being won. Heat eleven of the Oxford match saw what a simple mistake could have an effect. With Oxford's Chris Mills taking a tactical ride for double points his partner barker was well in the lead until he realised his team-mate was a long way back and Barker slowed down to a crawl to try and let him pass to gain two extra points, but Mildenhall's Armstrong was the winner and as the two Oxford riders crossed the line together the referee awarded second place to Barker and the tactical rider just one point to the cheers of the home crowd. This was now a critical part of the season as the Tigers strove to grab three more trophies for their hard work. Jon Armstrong flew the Mildenhall colours in the Yorkshire Junior Open Championship at Hull and took the honours after winning a run-off for the championship with Joel Parsons; no mean feat as his opponents was on his home track. Another double-header saw Buxton and Coventry beaten in two Trophy matches with Adam Roynon back from injury, only to lose him once again with an injured shoulder, which kept him out again. Together with Lee Smart Adam had been selected for the British Under 18 championship meeting at Wolverhampton

The first Sunday in October gave the fans yet another double headed meeting as Mildenhall firstly took on Oxford in the League - winning 55-37 - then the meeting was due to be taken over by the British Under 15's Final. The only Mildenhall rider in this event being Kyle Hughes. As it was the good old British weather took over and the second half was washed out and put on as part of another two-fixture meeting the next weekend. The first morsel was the Bronze Helmet meeting under the management of the legendary Bert Harkins, who had donated this trophy to the Conference League. This meeting brought together some of the top riders in the League and riders from most teams. The set-up saw the meeting down to two semi-finals which brought two riders to the tapes for the final run-off, this proving a winner in Jon Armstrong who beat Mark Burrows for the trophy.

After a long interval in trying to fix in the away leg of the KO Cup at Oxford it suddenly materialised one Friday evening when Mildenhall went to Oxford in a last minute dash, which saw them progress to the final which was to be the last meeting of the season at West Row. By this time, the Fen Tigers had already taken the Conference League championship for the second year in succession and the League Trophy.

After a good performance in the first leg away, the Fen Tigers faced the Boston Barracuda Braves for the finale at West Row. This proved to be a rather damp squib as on a damp evening, when after heat five and the Tigers 21-10 in the lead the Boston side protested that the track was too bad to ride any more, but when the referee took an inspection and said it was safe to carry on the Boston team walked out of the meeting. The Mildenhall riders had to go through the farce of riding each heat out for a 5-0 each time to win the Cup. This also after some trouble had erupted near the pits and which was quickly brought under control

Look back at the riders who did this (main ones); Richie Hawkins was well worthy of his captains role and a great inspiration to the younger

-93-

riders, also becoming the British Under 21 Champion in the meeting at Rye House, and went on to the World Under 21 Championships in Poland. He also had several rides for Berwick in the Premier League. *Jason King. It was to Mildenhall's advantage that he did not find a* Premier League spot and showed his ability throughout the season. Tony Dart was given a place in the Tigers team in only his second season in the sport; he was Mr Entertainment but took his riding more seriously when needed. James Mann came into the Fen Tigers quite late in the season after a long time on the injured list and was getting back to his best.

In his second year at West Row James Brundle made a remarkable recovery from a serious car crash, made a lot of progress during this season, and will always look upon Mildenhall as the track where he began his speedway career. Although he left to join Premier League Kings Lynn, Paul Lee had done his bit to see the League Championship come to Mildenhall, for whom he signed on sixteenth birthday. Kyle Hughes was signed on his fifteenth birthday and a very keen youngster who has a long career ahead of him in the speedway world. Lee Smart is also a very talented young rider who had already been selected for his country, and probably rode in more meetings than anyone else in 2004, and was determined to reach the top. Brought into the Mildenhall fold when Lee departed Jon Armstrong was a fantastic addition to the Tigers line-up, and an ultra professional. Another bright youngster was Adam Roynon who certainly has a bright future in front of him. Recovered from two separate injuries to ride in the last meeting of the year, Gary PhelpsA started in the Premier League at Edinburgh but struggled and came to Mildenhall, but after a bright start, an injury forced him to miss much of the latter part of the season.

Looking back over the previous three years, Mildenhall had possibly the best three seasons ever. It began in 2002 when they won the Conference League Trophy, and then followed this up with the League Championship and the Conference KO Cup in 2003. The 2004 season surpassed this with the Fen Tigers taking the Conference League honours for the second season in a row, adding the KO Cup once again and the League Trophy, and of course, they provided the Four-Team Champions as well. Graham Drury paid tribute to all those who work

hard behind the scenes to keep Mildenhall Speedway on the right track, and most of all to the supporters who had travelled far and wide once again to support their team up and down the country, sometimes nearly taking over opposing tracks with their happy approach to the meetings.
****

2005

What could actually follow the history-making season? The first thing is to look at the last team of riders for 2004 and then the seven that represented the Fen Tigers for the opening meeting of 2005. Instantly there is seen only two riders remain from the season before, Jon Armstrong who was promoted to captain the side, and a popular choice it was too, and young Adam Roynon who was now in the main body of the team after his fine displays of the previous year. However, most of all was the new company running speedway at West Row. After three years with Mildenhall Graham Drury and wife Denise decided to seek pastures new and take on another challenge at Workington. After some negotiation in came Peterborough based Mick Horton as the club owner, Neil Watson the club administrator, Trevor Swales the new chairman, and Wayne Swales as general manager as well as the team manager to take over the reigns. The full title this season was the UK Fire Fen Tigers. New owner Mick Horton announced, "I'll take Mildenhall into the Premier League in 2006."

The Conference League also made some important changes to their rules for the new season, probably through the success of the Fen Tigers over the last two years, although nobody actually said this was so. A brand new grading system was brought into being and effectively ensuring that the feats of Mildenhall may never be repeated. This system at least meant that most all the teams in the League start the season on a level playing field, to coin a phase. As it was, some bargains were there for the taking as some riders slipped through the net while others were set averages well above their stations; but it was something new to keep speedway to the forefront of British sport.

Out from the Conference League went Newcastle who moved up to the Premier League, Swindon disappeared , while little Carmarthen after being denied their track by the owners of the United Counties Showground had to take a year off from speedway. Coming back into the League were Scunthorpe who took the name the Scorpions, riding a brand new track at Normanby Road and topping their list of riders with two ex Fen Tigers in Wayne Carter and Ricky Scarboro, plus young 17-year-old South African Byron Bekker. Also stepping back into the Conference after eight years away was Sittingbourne Crusaders, who did ride in just the Conference League KO Cup the preceeding season. This was a new name for the Iwade training track, which had been in existence for many years.

All the usual competitions were working once more in the Conference League but with the Trophy being split into two sections more or less north and south of four teams each. The top two sides going into the semi-finals; while the bronze helmet was continued as per last year. As for league points, a bonus point was on offer when the aggregate scores - home and away - were added up and the point went to the team in front overall. For Mildenhall a coach was to be provided for some of the away meetings once again, being one of the few teams who take plenty of away supporters on a regular basis.

Lining up alongside Armstrong and Roynon were James Horton who was making a comeback into speedway after an enforced absence of a year, serving a suspension by the Speedway Control Board, plus a£500 fine, for testing positive for drugs after a Peterborough versus Mildenhall match in September 2003. Mark Thompson, was returning to the Fen Tigers once again, Scott Campos, after a few rides last year, and new names Gareth Hicknott, James   Purchase and the number eight was Bevan Gilbert-Jarrett. The new promoters stated their intentions early on when they said the new idea was to set the young riders on the right course to progressing further up the ladder, and not necessary to win trophies. Of course, if something were there to be won they would not turn it down. News of former Mildenhall riders saw Paul Lee in the Elite League with Peterborough Panthers and James Brundle had gone full time for Kings Lynn in the Premier League. Somerset was the place for Jason King, who also paraded Lee Smart in their team.

The Fen Tigers started with the all familiar challenge match at Boston that resulted in a defeat 52-44, but no so bad for a nearly new team, and away from home as well. The opening home meeting saw the touring

USA Dream Team, who was on a six-match tour. Laurence Rogers who was the touring team manager made this possible. The American riders, all based in California, were putting themselves in the shop window for the British clubs to have a look at, and a possible chance to ride in the countries speedway. It was a good test for Mildenhall who finally won 49-41 with Armstrong gaining a maximum twelve from his four rides and Roynon reaching double figures, and Chris Kerr top scoring for the Dream Team. Hicknott was not up to speed for the Tigers and drew a blank.

The second meeting at West Row was the British Under 21 Qualifier where some of the talented young riders, who were the lifeblood and the future of British speedway, were on sho w. The only Mildenhall riders taking part were Adam Roynon and Scott Campos, but James Horton was down as the meetings reserve rider. Of these, none of them went through although Adam Roynon narrowly missed out when his machine let him down at a vital moment. The winner of the meeting was Ben Wilson the nineteen-year-old from Sheffield, with a five-ride maximum while two of last years Fen Tigers James Brundle and Jason King got through. Also in the field were two former Fen Tigers in Barrie Evans and Lee Smart. Swindon's Conference League side included ex Tiger Kyle Hughes while Tony Dart had signed for Sittingbourne.

By the time that the third home meeting came along two Tigers had bit the dust, Gareth Hicknott and Bevan Gilbert-Jarrett having been dropped from the immediate plans. In came freshly signed riders 19-year-old Steve Braidford who had some Premier experience with Reading and Chris Geer, Steve unfortunately took a hard knock when riding at Weymouth and in spite of agreeing to ride at West Row he did not appear in the side at all, as he decided to concentrate on grass-track. He had ridden against Mildenhall in 2002 for Wolverhampton. Aiden Collins also put pen to paper in time for the next home meeting. He joined Mildenhall on loan from Workington and had experience in the Premier League. Chris Geer had been at Mildenhall in 2001 and in between at Sittingbourne and Wimbledon, and came to the Tigers with a two-point grade so was to fit in at reserve and so kick start his career again.

When the League trip to Buxton was postponed, the return challenge match was arranged as old friends Boston Barracuda Braves visited, and were looking to win back some pride after the last meeting in the Cup last season. It was also pleasing to see Malcolm Vasey back at West Row after his great help in the nineties to keep Mildenhall going in their meagre days. It was not to be however as after an even halfway point the Tigers gained victory by 46-42; the best thing being a large crowd who were entertained fully. Once again Jon Armstrong was unbeaten by an opposing rider, but poor James Horton had three falls, but showed what he could do by winning the other heat he was in. In all there were nine falls in the meeting, surprisingly six of them were on their home track. Another unfortunate problem came off the track when the public address system decided to play up, but with great effort the announcer Nick Knowles, got through most of the time. As with all new things, there were some Mildenhall supporters who were quick to tell people of little things not quite right, but by the time the serious meetings start these began to disappear. In addition, the very experienced presenter Kevin Long joined the staff.

Rye House and Mildenhall was the usual high standard meeting at Hoddesdon, with the home riders just edging out their visitors by 47-42, but Mildenhall pointed to an injury to Mark Thompson in his first ride as an upset. A last minute replacement was Karl White coming in for Horton, but the riders gave it All. This narrow defeat gave Mildenhall a very good chance to grab the bonus point in their home return meeting with the Rockets.

Then came to opening home league match when Newport Mavericks were the visitors. Since winning the league back in 1999 they had been struggling, but came to West Row after a win over Rye House Raiders (56-38) at home in Wales. Of the eighteen meeting of the two clubs, Fen Tigers and Newport, Mildenhall have won ten of them. Neil Watson found himself as team manager for this one, and debut rider Aiden Collins reeled off four straight wins as did Mark Thompson in a 54-37 win.

A week later, the visitors were the illustrious Wimbledon, managed by old Fen Tiger chief Dingle Brown, and one of the longest serving speedway clubs in the country. The Fen Tigers found themselves very short of riders with a lot of switching around Hicknott came back into the team and when Aidan Collins was unexpectedly recalled by Workington his parent club, time was short, and as a result Wimbledon went home with a 48-42 win, three falls and an engine failure did not help Mildenhall, although skipper Armstrong top scored with fourteen. An unusual feature of this meeting was that the last seven heats were all shared, and the Fen Tigers solitary heat win in the whole meeting. It was a just revenge for the two defeats suffered at the hands of Mildenhall last season. On top of all that Wimbledon's number one, and former Fen Tiger, Australian Scott James was late in arriving and missed his first ride. This unexpected home defeat saw some disagreement appear within the new promotion; on one hand, it was hoped that Mildenhall could bring through the ranks some of its home-grown riders, and on the other, the idea was to obtain the best riders available to help more silverware on the Tigers shelf. Compromises were made but by this time, the Mildenhall assets were out on loan. Jason King had signed for Somerset; Chris Schramm was with Berwick while Danny Betson joined Scunthorpe. The recall to Workington of Aiden Collins certainly did not help matters as during the twenty-eight days he was back in the north-west, he was not even included in the Workington squad, but they suddenly wanted him again to cover an injured rider. Mildenhall had him in their team at least for the visit of Armadale Devils

After James Horton had taken two more spills and getting just a single point it was a surprise when he d ecided to take a rest from the sport for a while. Adam Roynon was rewarded for his fine Tigers form with a guest ride at Kings Lynn, and skipper Armstrong rode for Peterborough versus Eastbourne and Oxford as a guest with great success. Horton however decided to switch to Boston, but after just one match and another injury he was out of the team and decided retirement was the option after all. That is until he turned up in the Mildenhall team later in the same year. Yet another puzzle was the fact that Steve Braidford was proving an invisible man as he was sought out for a possible return to the track.

The weather saw the two arranged meetings away at Wimbledon being called off, which was more than likely to the Tigers benefit as they strove to solve their early problems. The next home match was the visit of the 'Dale Devils' from Armadale in Scotland, the league leaders at the time, and was unique in one way that they fielded a team of which none of them had been a Fen Tiger before riding in Scotland. The visitors were virtually a two-man team, only Blair Scott and Derek Sneddon reaching double figures as Mildenhall won 51-44, James Purchase winning two heats from the reserve berth. Heat eleven threw up a scoreline of 7-0 to the visitors as both Tigers fell as Armadale took a tactical ride. A rumour also linked Andrew Bargh with Mildenhall but chairman Trevor Swales soon stopped that saying they would never poach another rider without permission.

The Fen Tigers supporters club w as still to the forefront in membership and had several activities on the move, including a free children's draw each week, a signed birthday card, and helping the rider's fuel bills and the Riders Equipment Fund, their annual assist. New this year was also a Lucky Chance Draw for one pound each week. Perry was also on the ball with coach trips to away meetings, some being away overnight and taking in two Mildenhall away meetings.

Three weeks went by before the next meeting when Wimbledon were the visitors once again, this time in the Conference Trophy. The break saw some strengthening of the Tigers line-up. For quite a while Steve Braidford had proved extremely illusive to contact, and had become known as the 'invisible man' and so he was dropped from the squad to make way for Tony Dart, who had to delay his debut as he was in America on business. Collins was thought to be available again, while Lee Smart re-joined from Weymouth with team-mate Matt Bates. Weymouth had suddenly switched their operation night to Friday, which clashed with Somerset and Smarts riding for them. Unfortunately Bates had a bad crash in his second ride when he got tangled up on the second bend, badly injuring his back, and when Campos also withdrew as well, battered and bruising the leg he broke the previous year, following heavy crash, the Tigers were left with just five fit riders who pulled out all the stops to take the win 51-42, an amazing performance, also considering they could only put out one rider in heats eight and ten. Holding Wimbledon together was reserve Danny Betson, a Fen Tigers asset, who crammed in seven rides for his eighteen points, nearly half the Dons total. A quick return visit to Wimbledon in the league, with a six-man team - Adam being unavailable - saw the Fen Tigers beaten by only four points50-46. Lee Smart and Jon Armstrong were outstanding each collecting nineteen points, and young Trevor Heath making his first appearance for the Tigers at reserve.

Stoke Spitfires were next up at West Row and in their side was Barrie Evans a former Fen Tiger who was once the club little mascot. In the Mildenhall 54-41 win, Armstrong posted his first maximum (15) of the season with Heath on his first home match, registering a useful two paid four for his troubles. Stoke's near novice reserve pair had a bad afternoon as in their eight rides they fell four times and were last in three more. On the other hand, Stokes two tactical rides produced the full points. A slight disagreement in the camp meant this fixture was the last one for Adam Roynon as he had decided to seek pastures new. It was a time also to change the front cover of the Mildenhall programme from the ring of team members to an action photograph, the original riders pictured had suddenly become out of date and a new team picture was taken as the original had suffered the same fate.

Entering June an away match at Boston saw Mildenhall go down 51-41. The six-man team - Aiden Collins was missing again - owed much of their total to a super human performance by captain Jon Armstrong, who totaled nineteen points, nearly half the teams score, and as a result the scores were kept at a reasonable ten points gap. Jon had been in double figures in every meeting so far this year, indeed a clear case of the skipper leading from the front.

Right in the middle of league and trophy meetings Mildenhall filled up a blank Sunday at the last minute, by entertaining Buxton in a challenge match. To help the track staff get the track ready in time some early arriving supporters got down to it and leant a hand in putting the safety fence up; great fans these people were. The chance was taken in this meeting to introduce another new rider Chris Johnson, who opened his account with a paid nine. However, reserve James Purchase and Mark Thompson were hit with injuries and missed the next two meetings. For the visit to Scunthorpe T, Webster came in at reserve in the six-man team, but they went down 50-43. Another good sign was young reserve Matt Bates out with injury, going along as well to help cheer the team on. Weymouth came to West Row next having won twelve of their last thirteen matches, while the Tigers included another new face in Andrew Bargh, having switched to the fens from Wimbledon, who had suspended him for a while over his move. In the 49-43 win Armstrong notched up sixteen points with double figures from Smart and new boy Bargh in the sweltering sun. Heat six provided one of the closest finishes as Armstrong swept past Dan Gifford on the final bend. Another change in the Tigers camp was Mick Horton taking over the post of team manager from Wayne Swales.

One innovation was the holding of a 'fans forum' after some home meetings, held after the match, in which anyone could come along with their questions. Coach trips planned included a two-day trip to Weymouth that was fully booked after just two weeks. This trip gave the Tigers supporters a day out at the seaside as well. That Fen Tigers supporters are one of the most loyal bunch in speedway circles there is no doubt and they showed their appreciation to their riders by a collection of over two hundred pounds for the injured Matt Bates. It was time also for teams in the Conference League to swap around riders as some were dropped and others signed to try to create a winning team, and to this end Sittingbourne Crusaders were found short very quickly and two ex Mildenhall riders appeared in their colours, in the shape of Darren Andrews and Ricky Scarboro.

The Conference League Four Team Championship took place at Loomer Road, Stoke, and Weymouth came out on top, but only one point in front of Oxford. Mildenhall went out in the semi-finals with ten points, which left them bottom of semi-final two; Armstrong, Collins, Smart and Bargh being their riders. The League decreed a change in the way the four riders were selected, the team being built around the 32-point limit and the reserves for each team had to be from the Stoke camp who was hosting the meeting.

The danger that was Boston were next up at West Row in the Trophy, led as ever by their excitable boss Malcolm Vasey, and Roynon also made a quick return in the Barracuda's colours. This was the seventy-first meeting of these two local rivals of which Mildenhall had won thirty-seven and Boston twenty-nine. It proved quite a highly charged match with Mildenhall certainly not helped when Armstrong - after two heat wins - and Scott Campos were both withdrawn from the meeting after heat ten, and after the Tigers had been ten points in front at one time. Boston took full advantage to gain a victory by 49-42. Aidan Collins made a surprising home appearance but also fell twice after a win and two second places in his first three heats. In the race to keep on the bikes for the four laps Mildenhall won that contest by four falls to the Barracuda Braves three.

With Collins absent rider-replacement was used for the long trek down to Weymouth, who sent the Tigers home with their tail between the legs with a 56-37 mauling, by one of the favourites to win the league. A powerful Oxford seven were the next Sunday visitors to West Row in what was the Fen Tigers two hundredth Conference League meeting since they re-joined in 1994, and it could be said they were robbed of a win, the match ending all square at 46 each. Joel Parsons, the Aussie from Broken Hill, had joined up with the Fen Tigers from Hull his Premier club, but after four points from his first two rides, he was sent sprawling into the fence by Oxford's Ben Barker, and suffered multiple fractures to his leg. This put him out of action for the rest of the season, and for a while Mildenhall seriously considered further action against the Oxford rider.

Sittingbourne Crusaders were finding the going tough and were at the foot of the league table when they came to visit with their captain Andre Cross, who once rode some second-halves at West Row, and three others with Tiger connections, Darren Andrews, Gary Phelps and James Theobald. The visitors provided only two heat winners, strangely enough in the first two heats, as Mildenhall won 63-30. They quickly followed this up with a nail-biting away victory at Boston 49-44, and although losing at Weymouth the Fen Tigers won away again, this time at a bright and breezy Buxton by 51-39. These two away wins came after a long run of defeats on their travels by the Fen Tigers, as the saying about buses goes 'after a long wait two came along at once'. The Conference League Pairs at Wimbledon saw the Mildenhall pairing - Armstrong and Smart - finish in second place in the semi-finals with eight points but were not in the final. Jon blowing up his engine just before the meeting was not the best of times as he was forced to use his other bike, which was set up for a longer track, of which Plough Lane is definitely not that kind. Then a return visit by Oxford for the Knockout Cup, in the height of the summer was rained-off. The Fen Tigers did however have a fixture to turn out for, when they attended the local Mildenhall Carnival. This was to further advertise their meetings; three riders plus the team managers were asked many questions during the day. A familiar figure in the pits helping his son Trevor Heath was his father, and it was a shock for everyone when he suddenly collapsed and passed away on 24 July; a two minutes silence was observed at the next home meeting.

When Weymouth came to West Row for the second time, this time for league points, they were still one of the teams looking to top the league, but Mildenhall did it once more by winning 56-31. The Wildcats were hampered by Gifford falling in his first race and withdrawing from the meeting, still another good win. Six of the Mildenhall riders won a heat with Mark Thompson top scoring with thirteen points. Top scorer for the visiting team was the Welsh Wizard Tom Brown, and at reserve was Jack Gledhill the son of Ian, a one time Fen Tiger.

Mildenhall continued to be the only side to have a consistent group of their supporters at the away meetings, sometimes a full coach of fans made the longer trips to Wales and Scotland. This was done with the help of supporters joining a 'Travel Club' which gave them first choice and reduced fares for the journey's, all this under the expert eye of Perry the 'Coach Arranger', who had a special date of his own when he got wed to Marie.

This was quickly followed by old favourites Rye House at West Row, although the programme tried to fool us by quoting the date as the thirteenth of August instead of the fourteenth. Although boss Len Silver fielded a strong team, they only had two heat wins, both by their New Zealander Ben Powell as the Tigers recorded one of their biggest victories over the Hertfordshire side, 51-39. All seven Mildenhall riders registered a heat win, which included Trevor Heath registering his first winning ride for the Tigers. It was pleasing in the pits to see everyone helping each other and Lee Smart's father Malcolm moving around giving a hand to who ever needed it. Over the years these meetings were always very close and up to this time the Fen Tigers had won 34 times and Rye House 29; even the points were near - 2764 to Mildenhall and 2725 to Rye House.

A healthy win at Sittingbourne meant that Mildenhall moved to the top of the Conference League table, but they had ridden more meetings than all the rest. This was only for a short time as Oxford were still the favourites to end as champions, but the Tigers were on hand to pick up on any slip up by the Oxford machine. Many people however put down Weymouth as the likely champions although they had some fixtures in hand over their opponents and had to win these to top the table. Bad news for the Tigers however came when Chris Johnson broke his collarbone when riding for Reading, but James Horton was making yet another try to come back into the sport after suffering a time of injuries reaching back almost to the start of the season. He looked on top of the situation with a steady score of paid seven against Rye House.

A 57-39 victory over Boston Barracuda Braves meant Mildenhall had won six out of the last seven matches and looked to be on for a grandstand finish. The visitors however were missing two top riders who were with their Premier League sides, and two injuries, but to their credit, they never thought once about trying to postpone the meeting and just got on with it. Fate seemed to be against them in the first two heats when Mallett was disqualified for having no guard on the rear wheel and Richardson was in trouble for a tapes offence. In fact, they did pick up double points twice in the meeting through ex-Tiger Wayne Dunworth and Darren Mallett. Mark Thompson had a good meeting against one of his former teams as he notched up four heat wins for Mildenhall. Once more, the programme printers caused some confusion when the details of the Boston riders were put under the heading of Rye House riders; still something to do for the supporters - looking for the deliberate mistakes - or not as the case may be. We also had the distinction of having two meetings labelled 'Number eighteen' in two successive weeks against two different teams, before the needle righted itself and moved on to meeting nineteen. Hey Ho! Putting on the track the same seven in two consecutive meetings was a luxury and promoter Mick Horton tempted fate by announcing they were close to having a settled team, and so deep into the season as well!

With Mildenhall challenging in the top half of the league they looked ahead and the chance of injuries upsetting things, so they went out and signed Paul Burnett as a back up system, who joined the squad. The KO Cup Quarter-Final came up next when Oxford were the opponents at West Row, and threw up a track problem after the first heat when the referee Dave Dowling ordered the re-grading of the second bend as it was thought to be dangerous, so the meeting took a long enforced break while the track staff got to work. This was eventually carried out to the referee's satisfaction and everything got underway once more. Straightaway Oxford's Sam Martin reared at the start and was taken off in the ambulance, taking no further part in the meeting. The bulk of the visitors points came from the Branney brothers John and Craig, who between them notched up thirty of Oxford's total of forty. Mildenhall however scored regularly all round to take a lead of fourteen points into the deciding away leg.

Mildenhall's title bid hit the dust in some style during September when four away meetings in succession were all lost, these being league fixtures at Newport, where a sizable lead was given away, Armadale and Oxford, although they kept the score down in the KO Cup at Oxford to reach the semi-final on aggregate where old friends Boston awaited them. The two Oxford meetings were held on the same day, one after the other, this was to help Oxford to get their fixtures completed. Newcomer Paul Burnett rode twice scoring 12 in the first match but then dropped to just 2, while Chris Johnson was missing through injury.

The Fen Tigers on their own patch had beaten the Buxton Hitmen earlier in the year, so Mildenhall were looking for the double and the bonus point on offer. They took the win by 59-36 and in doing so provided the heat winner in fourteen of the fifteen heats. It must be said though that Buxton lost their number seven Ross Parker, when he took a big tumble in the warm-up practice, and withdrew from the meeting. Back from injury, Chris Johnson got a paid maximum, and Andrew Bargh weighed in with four heat wins. It was also a day for the older Tigers supporters when, after the meeting Shane Henry, the son of former Mildenhall favourite Robert Henry, had a few laps together with his father to bring back the tears of nostalgia of yesteryear for those who stopped behind to witness this attention-grabbing event. A demonstration in sidecar racing was another second half attraction; it had been paraded back in the 2001 season and in being tried out again, it was being thought of as a regular attraction.

Yet another side to visit Mildenhall and proved to be virtually a two-man team was Scunthorpe, for whom ex-Fen Tiger and veteran Wayne Carter mustered up nineteen points from his six rides, and he was helped in his cause by Ricky Scarboro who turned in a double figure score; Mildenhall winning 57-37. In addition, an afternoon of team riding saw Fen Tigers riders sweep up eight bonus points between them. It was also on this day that the speedway world was rocked when it became known that the famous old team Wimbledon would be closing down after a great deal of years in the sport; almost from the beginning. The Greyhound Racing Association, who own Plough Lane, had massively increased the rent for the speedway team, and not being able to raise the huge amount were faced with closure.

One thing that never changed at Mildenhall is giving the youngsters a chance in the sport and it showed in the list of riders for this season. Only once did they resort to bringing in a guest rider, Karl White (Rye House) preferring to bring in riders just starting out. In finishing fourth, they had seven riders who boasted an average of eight or over, top being Jon Armstrong with over nine points. With this in mind it was announced that Mildenhall had applied to move up to the Premier League but also to continue running a team in the Conference League as well.

The re-erected Bronze Helmet meeting attracted some of the top Conference riders, with the home riders Lee Smart and Jon Armstrong - who was defending his title won last year - waving the Fen Tigers flag. Armstrong reached the semi-finals but then missed the gate and lost his chance of repeating the previous year's triumph, Jamie Courtney going into the final. However, the Bronze Helmet winner being the young 15-year-old Lewis Bridger from Weymouth. This meeting was shared with the British Under-15 Championship (Final Round) which numbered an exciting list of young riders, hoping to make their mark in the sport.

Once again, Boston provided the opposition for the KO Cup semi-final second leg, the Fen Tigers having already built up a ten-point lead from the 1st leg at Boston. A score of 60-33 to Mildenhall - the second time they had topped sixty points this season - saw them progress safely to the final, with James Purchase top scoring with 13 +2 from the reserve berth, after Chris Johnson had crashed out of the meeting in his first ride. It was left to Darren Mallett to carry the Boston team with sixteen points, almost half of his team's total. The Steve Heath Memorial Trophy took the second half of the meeting. Steve was the father of young Trevor and had supported him in his efforts to break into the speedway world; also taking a prominent part at Eastbourne's training track for the youngsters. This Trophy was for the best pairs, which included some top class guests from the Premier League. Among these was Hungarian Norbert Magosi who had been with Peterborough in 2004 but had not ridden in England in 2005 and was looking for a team for the next season. Coming out top of the bunch was Andrew Bargh with Danny King the Ipswich rider in the Elite League.

A big deficit from their first leg of the KO Cup Final at Weymouth proved just that bit too much for the Fen Tigers to overcome in their home leg, and Weymouth took the Trophy although they lost the second leg 51-45. Three of their riders scored eleven points, Bridger, Mason and Gifford. After this meeting, the body colours of the Mildenhall team were auctioned off, duly signed by each rider; proving a great opportunity to collect some Fen Tigers history. For the record Mildenhall finished in third place in the Conference League, a high position considering the silly matches given away during a busy season.

For Mildenhall there was something to celebrate being their 30th Anniversary and a special night of racing, plus a gathering of some of the old faces who had made Mildenhall the great little speedway track and club it had become. The format of the evenings racing was four 4-men teams competing, and as no names had been suggested for these they were simply named teams A,B,C and D. While it did not really matter who won and who lost, for the record it was team C (Daniel King, Jon Armstrong, Richie Hawkins Lee Smart) who took the honours. The Premier League riders who were appearing included Shaun Tacey (Workington), James Brundle (Kings Lynn), Daniel King

(Ipswich), Richie Hawkins (Somerset) and Sean Wilson (Sheffield).

To wind up the proceedings the former riders of Mildenhall were large in number and it would take another page to list them all. Safe to say they included in their midst favourites such as Ray Bales, Mick Bates (now a top speedway referee), Carl Blackbird, Gavin Hedge, Robert Henry (popular captain of the champions in 1979), Mick & Andy Hines, Kevin Jolly, Roger Pascall (one of the oldest riders from the first season), Mel Taylor. There were not only riders but also those who made Mildenhall click when they were at West Row. Dingle Brown (promoter in late 1990's), David Gage (timekeeper for many years), Dick Partridge (promoter 1992), Graham Drury (successful promoter) Colin Barber (original promotion member) and former world champions Michael Lee who started at the track in a field with straw bales in 1974.

****

2006

The long promised season arrived and the dawn of a new era, with Mildenhall stepping up to the Premier League to pit their strength against the supposed better teams. But they did not leave the Conference League altogether as they were running a team in that division, and were to be known as the Mildenhall Academy, the youngsters being sponsored as a team by 'Jolly Chef' a well known local catering business. The Premier League team were under the banner of 'ASL Freight' Fen Tigers.

Premier League side was Jason Lyons, Shaun Tacey as captain, Daniel King, Jason King, James Brundle, Barry Burchett and the only one of last season's side Jon Armstrong. Probably the best signing was Lyons who was an Australian rider with a great deal of experience and had ridden thirty-eight times for his country, and had been a regular rider in the Grand Prix series. He certainly showed his pedigree as he steered his way without any seemingly effort round the small Mildenhall circuit. Tacey had been making the long trip each week to Workington from his Norwich base and welcomed the chance to ride nearer home.

The Conference League side included Mark Thompson, Andrew Bargh, Mark Baseby, Trevor Heath, Ben Hopwood and James Purchase. Danny Norton was named as the seventh rider and captain but in the first outing versus the USA Dream Team he was missing from the line-up and replaced by Matt Wright. The youngest member of the Academy was Hopwood who only turned fifteen on the eve of the season, but had been having rides after the second half at Belle Vue. Gone were Lee Smart to Plymouth, and Chris Johnson to IOW. The team manager was Blayne Scroggins.

On Sunday 5 March 2006, the Fen Tigers opened the season with a Challenge match against long-term local side Rye House who had been Premier League champions the previous season; this was termed the Suffolk/Herts Cup for want of a better title. This did much to show how good the Mildenhall team was as they went down 47-43 to the reigning titleholders with Danny King showing the way for the Tigers with four wins and a second place to top score with fourteen points. With two heats left, the scores were level so this result was better than it looks on paper.

A new venture by the supporters was the Fen Tigers 100 Club, set up to allow the fans to support the riders by giving £10 each month throughout the season. For this subscription, a monthly draw was to take place at a home meeting where one member would be the winner of 10% of that month's sponsorship money. The Supporters Club was still in operation as well, under the guidance of Linda, Di and Janet. Yet another new venture was to take place at the end of the season when the Mildenhall Premier League Race Suits were to be signed and auctioned off to the highest bidders.

The following two meetings were away. At Rye House where they lost once again, the score this time being 50-41 The scores had remained close after eight heats but all things changed when a trainee referee took control and by heat fourteen the meeting had become a near farce as some very strange decisions were made and some of the riders on both sides were confused. Danny King scored 28 points in the two meetings v Rye House but most alarming was the non-scoring Shaun Tacey at Rye House.

Next a visit to Elite League Ipswich for an Inter-League Challenge on an extremely cold night, the home team being victorious by 54-40.

Honorary Tigers for the night being Chris Neath and Stuart Robson in place of Armstrong and Burchatt; this after the BSPA in its wisdom had stepped in to prevent Mildenhall from bringing in Elite League guests to make a better match of it. The racing in this meeting was processional with even the top riders finding it difficult to try and passing. Facing Ipswich in the return at West Row the Fen Tigers matched their visitors almost to the end, providing eight heat winners to Ipswich's seven, and only four points divided the teams at the end (47-43). Many of the large crowd said it was the best meeting for some considerable time at West Row.

A fortnight into the new season and following four defeats, albeit to two paramount sides, the visit of Isle of Wight to Mildenhall in the Premier Trophy was the first major meeting of the season , and Mildenhall started well with a 58-34 victory; Danny King, Jon Armstrong and Shaun Tacey putting up double figure scores. The scores were quite level until the second half of the match when the Tigers pulled clear. A trip to Somerset came next where the Tigers did not get a feel for the track early on, but once they adapted they more than held their own and only went down by just seven points, which was proficient for that track. One gripe from a travelling Tigers fan was the fact that only two of their riders came round to acknowledge the supporters who had made the effort to support the team on their travels. On to Newport where the Fen Tigers gained a well-merited draw of forty-five each; a meeting that also could have easily been won by the visitors.

The South Wales side were the next at West Row and Jason Lyons lit up the track with a perfect five-ride maximum in a 49-40 Mildenhall victory, while Danny King dropped just one point to the opposition. This meeting was the first of several double-headers when the second match up was the Mildenhall Academy faced the USA Dream Team and got off to a start to the season with a win as James Purchase, Matt Wright and Mark Thompson all reached double figures. Another signing for the Academy was Luke Goody who had just taken to speedway from grass-track racing. Another young rider with a familiar name took a ride after the meeting had finished; Jake Knight son of ex-Tiger Richard. A Trophy match against Rye House saw the Fen Tigers avenge the challenge match defeat by sending the Rockets home pointless (46-44) after the Tigers had been behind after thirteen heats, coming good late on to snatch the win, and this with only six heat winners. Somerset also went the same way as Mildenhall began to feel their feet in higher company (54-41).

Sad news that Brian Snowie passed away on 31 April. He was one of the most appreciated workers in the background of Mildenhall Speedway, his title of Commercial and Marketing manager and Youth Scout did not reflect on the many jobs he worked at for the Mildenhall club. This time it was an under statement when everyone said he will be sorely missed; it went without saying.

After a little war of words in the local newspapers the Fen Tigers faced Kings Lynn in a true derby match, which Mildenhall acquired 'bragging rights' for a while by being victorious by 49-44, in a meeting in which Jon Armstrong was on top form with fifteen points. The Academy team versus Stoke Spitfires followed this again, and the lead changed hands regularly until the visitors took the points with a last heat win to make the end score 44-46. The Fen Tigers Conference League side had started their away meetings with a heavy loss down the road at Rye House. Two Sunday meetings were then rained off before Kings Lynn paid their second visit to West Row, this time in search of Premier League points and this time they won a tight match by just two points, Lyons being Tigers top man at sixteen. A trip 'overseas' for Mildenhall saw them lose out to the Isle of Wight. Mildenhall also had a new man on view as Andrew Moore made his debut in place of Shaun Tacey, as the promotion took the decision to let the former captain go after not pasting up the scores he had been capable of. After two defeats, home and away to Boston, the Academy had suffered three meetings being postponed. Saddlebow Road was the venue of the |British Under 21 Final and taking part were the Tigers trio of Danny King, Jason King and James Brundle; however, Ben Wilson came out on top as Danny reached the final.

The Mildenhall Academy were kept quiet for much of May when six of their meetings were postponed and just three matches run, losing all three, and a very frustrating time. One thing on the up however were the

-112-

attendances at West Row plus some more sponsors coming forward, just what were needed to keep the Fen Tigers head above the water. Meanwhile the much-fancied Glasgow Tigers came to West Row and found the Mildenhall team at their best winning 49-44, Jason Lyons posting up a paid maximum. A disappointment was the retirement of Andrew Moore who decided after just one meeting that he could not afford to continue in the sport and losing money. The next week saw American Brent Werner coming in from Eastbourne and straight away was among the points in the 51-41 victory over Newcastle, and Joel Parsons standing in for Jason King.

After departing from the League KO Cup with the Tigers losing both legs of the meeting with Somerset, the Redcar Bears were next at West Row. Down in Somerset after the away meeting there were some mutterings from the Mildenhall supporters at the way the team manager had handled the tactical rides, many thought they could have done it better; doesn't this happen in every sport? Mildenhall were without Jon Armstrong against the Bears after a fall at Rye House the previous evening, and this just as he had moved into the Fen Tigers team proper at number two after some excellent meeting at the reserve berth. The Redcar riders were at their best and a close meeting ended with as share of the points at 45-45. Danny King took on the captain's armband for the Tigers.

There was another moan of the track not being up to the usual standard and again this was after a Stock Car Meeting the night before which cut into the surface more than usual on a damp night. Although this saw both speedway sides having problems and the Fen Tigers did not have the advantage a home team often has in meetings. The Conference League Fen Tigers were part of the meeting with a match versus Rye House second string, but continued a losing run by 58-32, although they lost Mark Thompson after one ride; he had been feeling unwell before the meeting started. . This was after a bright performance in the League Fours at Stoke and reached the final finishing third. Young Luke Goody had by now made his Conference League debut.

One of the better performances away from West Row saw a depleted team go down by only six points at Newcastle. With Rider Replacement for Armstrong, Jason King not available and a blank day for Burchett did not help but Craig Branney came in the team as a guest and rattled up ten good points. Then came three victories in a row for Mildenhall, a win at Somerset - the first success on the travels - was followed by two home successes over Isle of Wight and Edinburgh. The Somerset match was part of a two-day tour in the South-West and both meetings were very vocal from the Mildenhall travelling supporters that very often out shouted the home fans. Ben Powell rode for Mildenhall as a guest at IOW.

The Fen Tigers Academy went to Plymouth with virtually half a team but were helped out by Jordan Frampton and the debut boy Shane Henry, Jordan the son of Robert. Frampton then came into the side as a regular replacement for Burchett, sharing the berth with Powell now a Fen Tiger. Of much interest was the inclusion in the Plymouth team of woman rider Jessica Lamb in their home meeting. Mildenhall had a quick chance to turn the tables when Plymouth Devils came to West Row. Mildenhall won the reverse fixture 49-44 with a solid all-round showing. Shane helped out the visitors in this meeting, riding at number two.

The meeting at West Row saw the Fen Tigers extend their unbeaten home run to five meetings when the Potters were beaten 51-44. This meeting also included the Academy versus Rye House Raiders, a match which was lost 58-31. The youngsters having just four heat winners and ended up with only five fit riders. To their benefit, the Academy side had won well at Newport for their first away points of the season.

The Yorkshire Tigers were in town at the end of August when Sheffield were Mildenhall's opponents. Jon Armstrong was back after a prolonged rest due to injury; this meeting coming on the back of the Mildenhall win at Edinburgh, and the postponement of the Premier League Fours at Workington. In spite of a first-rate maximum of fifteen from Danny King, offset by a poor display in the reserve positions, Sheffield got the win, but only by a two-point margin. This saw the chance of a place in the play-off's virtually disappear for the Fen Tigers.

****

2007

There had been much going on during the winter break at Mildenhall Speedway, the main item coming from Lawrence Rogers who put a bid in to run the Fen Tigers, but this failed to materialise when one of his investors withdrew. Local accountant Simon Barton kept on board however and took the role of Financial Director in the new consortium, which included the West Row Stadium owner Carl Harris. Simon had been a Mildenhall supporter since their very early days. This new company also offered the fans the chance to buy into their club by purchasing shares, which many did. Rogers was the new Team Manager and owing to matters not being finalised until quite late the task of putting a team together was made harder. The Conference team was not to run this year, just the Premier League team.

Of last years team Jason King was the only survivor, so there were several new faces in the Tigers line-up for 2007, the vice-captain being Denmark's Tom P Madsen who had spent the previous season at Belle Vue, and who had made his British debut with Berwick in 1999 and had ridden for his country. The highly rated Canadian Kyle Legault also joined the Fen Tigers from Sheffield, and Czech Republic's Mario Jirout was back for the British season in the Tigers colours. Locally based Jamie Smith who had missed most of the 2006 season with a broken leg but was making a return with Mildenhall. At number seven was top Academy rider Mark Thompson while back to try once again was Shaun Tacey after last years nightmare.

The press and practise day proved very successful and even the day came out to shine on the new Fen Tigers, especially the management team resplendent in their new Tigers shirts, together with the mechanics also wearing the new colours, courtesy of the Supporters Club. Another closed doors practise took place the next day. It was not all roses however as three staff vehicles had some trouble on the press day, including start marshal David Bateman but old friend Kelvin Mullarkey got all things going again.

For their opening meeting Sheffield Tigers were met home and away in a challenge match dubbed the Top Tiger Trophy. This was a thrilling match on a cold and windy day, which saw the rain start after the fourth heat, but not enough to force an ending to the proceedings. Huggy back on the tractor provided a high-quality track and the match ended with both sides on forty-five points. In the second leg at Sheffield, the Fen Tigers lost out 59-31, but only after the home riders pulled away in the closing heats. The travelling Mildenhall supporters were acknowledged when the team came out to the centre green to thank them with a wave; nice touch. The second home meeting was the Premier Trophy match against Somerset and proved an exciting and sometimes-hard racing which saw Shaun and Mario shunted to one side in heat one but at the halfway point Mildenhall were six points in front. Heat thirteen then blew up and the Rebels captain and number one Magnus Zetterstrom was excluded for unfair riding, Madsen being the victim, but a 5-0 and 5-1 saw Mildenhall victorious by 54 to 38.

A meeting always looked forward to was the visit of Rye House, and Mildenhall had a stroke of luck; if you could call it that; when Tai Woffinden the Rye House rider in top form was withdrawn from the meeting after a second heat crash also involving Jason King. It was still a close match which saw Mildenhall victorious by one point (45-44). This was the first defeat suffered by Rye House and came after they had won well against Mildenhall (66-23) the night before at home. The Fen Tigers were proving bad travellers and their overseas trip to the Isle of Wight ended in another heavy loss 62-30. The Newport meeting was run on a Saturday afternoon at 2-30 and allowed those who wanted to also take in the Elite League Best Pairs at Kings Lynn in the evening.. The match with the Wasps ended after a ghastly crash that saw Jamie Smith flung right over the high fence on to the greyhound track in heat fourteen, this resulting in injuries which put him out of action for the second season in a row. This time it was reckoned to be at least three months before he could start to think about riding again. With the score standing at 52-34 when this happened this was to stand.

In place of Jamie it was decided to bring in some guest riders for the time being as riders with the same average were few on the ground, and for the meeting with Isle of Wight in came Stoke's Ben Barker. This turned out not to be the only change when Mario Jirout went down with tonsillitis so the Tigers operated rider replacement and Plymouth's Niki Glanz was at number eight; he was the son of former Mildenhall rider

Peter Glanz. The Fen Tigers rode their hearts out to gain a slender win by 47-46.

The Mildenhall Supporters Club was again going great guns with a super-sized raffle each home meeting, and a second effort looking to supplement the Riders Equipment Fund. The youngsters were not forgotten, as the winner of a separate competition would meet the rider of their choice and a picture taken with them. Away travel continued to be well supported and for the trip to the IOW some had to be turned away as the coach was packed full. To put the Fen Tigers more on the local map they had representatives and a rider at both the Isleham Carnival and the Globe Pub Bike Show, together with a campaign to have posters displayed in all the nearby towns to bring in more spectators. On top of the Supporters Clubs funds the Track staff got together and with collections each week among themselves, they were helping Tigers riders with problems with machinery

To cover for the injured Smith Mildenhall continued to bring in a guest in his place, as finding a rider with the right average permanently was proving difficult. Paul Cooper and Chris Johnson being the guest in the next two meetings. The KO Cup meeting at West Row against Rye House came to an abrupt end when in heat nine the visitors Stuart Robson rode full pelt into the safety fence. The long interlude in treating the rider meant there was no option but to abandon the meeting; Mildenhall were two points in front at the time but the match was to be re-run. In heat three, Tommy Allen of Rye House was also out of the rest of the meeting after a bad tumble. For the away leg that was then the first leg at Hoddesdon guest Tomas Suchanek registered a well-earned ten points as the Tigers went down 50-41; not a bad result as the Rockets had been beaten only once so far this season. It was then the turn of Mildenhall to lose a rider in his first race, who was advised to withdraw; this being Chris Johnson versus Redcar. Then it was the turn of Dan Gifford and James Cockle to fill the vacant space in the Tigers line-up for the next two matches. Cockle was having an adverse time at Sheffield and he said the Newcastle meeting was his best meeting so far this season.

There was a general upheaval in the Mildenhall camp and suddenly

Mario Jirout was left out of the team, the team manager commenting that he had badly let the team down on the visit to Glasgow, and would no longer be riding for the Fen Tigers.

As a result of this two new riders joined the Fen Tigers, Tomas Suchanek from Somerset and Paul Fry, the latter was opposite the original Mildenhall club was formed, for youngsters, Fry was a real speedway veteran at in his forties. They were down to make their debuts in the long awaited home meeting with Kings Lynn only for the Bank Holiday weather to spoil all the plans. But another clash to wet the apatite against Rye House in the KO Cup was next Unfortunately this saw a under par performance by Mildenhall to go down 49-40 after losing Tom P, and this after winning the opening heat; Suchanek top scoring with 12+1.

Sharing the stadium with other sports did not help on several occasions, and was shown by what the track staff found one Sunday morning after the Saturday night stock-car meeting. The track and its surrounds was littered with debris, and they had to clear broken cars, chassis, engines and various bits and pieces when they arrived at seven in the morning to get the track ready for the afternoon speedway. The actual track was bare and shale had to be dug out from under the fence to make the track fit for riding, but time was mostly against the willing helpers and sometimes the racing suffered because of the damage inflicted on it by the stack-cars. The Rye House meeting with a bumper crowd was one of those days with the heat (24 degrees it was said) and even Huggy had difficulty with the watering and other efforts to keep the riding up to standard. In the middle of June the use of the stadium on a Sunday by the Fen Tigers was put off as the fitting of a new greyhound rail was being fitted; oh well happy days!

The Stoke meeting showed the 'never say die' attitude of the Mildenhall team and after being behind for all the match they piled up two maximum heat wins (5-1) in the last two heats to grab the points 49-44; what an ending after all the troubles with the track and other problems. After the meeting, the Baseby brothers Aaron and Mark had a few laps.

Something had to be done about the state of the track however, and another postponed weekend gave the workers the time to clear more litter of cars and pieces. They had to completely re-lay the speedway track, which included 150 tonnes of fresh shale being carted in for use. Now it could be seen to help the speedway meetings along without hurried work trackside. The second postponement was down to a flooded track after some monsoon like weather leading up to the weekend. When the entire track preparing gang turned up on the Sunday morning they were faced with something resembling a river, so there was no question of racing later in the day. Kyle Legault was away the weekend in Grand Prix semi-final in Terenzano in Italy and done the Tigers proud with a points haul of eleven and qualified for the semi-finals which were the following weekend. Another Mildenhall rider Tomas Suchanek also flew the flag by qualifying for the European Championship Final.

The Saturday home meeting with Kings Lynn saw Theo Pijper as a guest for Leghault, while a change was made at reserve and after a long look at performances, young Mark Baseby was given a chance in place of Mark Thompson; the youngster was with Sittingbourne this year. Away at Newport on the Sunday, Lee Complin was due for a guest ride but had to pull out and Rusty Harrison came in his place. Local rivals Kings Lynn managed to get the meeting at West Row in but probably wished they had not when a splendid feat by the Fen Tigers saw them win 50-42. The elements then forced yet another postponement when only two heats were completed before heavy thunderstorm washed the meeting out

The Mildenhall trek north for matches at Edinburgh, Berwick and Newcastle was not a very good success on the track with defeats in Scotland and Newcastle and the Berwick meeting being put off. However, it was good for some team bonding at a ten-pin bowling night and then a party evening with the supporters at Berwick. One of the highlights of the tour was the efforts of Mark Baseby ending in a paid seven in the final meeting. Jamie Smith was also back on his bike after his bad crash and as the Tigers could not fit him in the team owing to the averages, he went to Stoke on loan. Into the Mildenhall squad came Nicki Glanz to share the reserve berth with Baseby, while still riding for

-119-

his Conference team Plymouth.

For the visit of Edinburgh, the Tigers tracked Daniel Halsey as a guest reserve but although trying hard failed to score, but double figure returned from Kyle, Jason and Tomas gave Mildenhall a 51-41 victory, just failing to grab the bonus point. Kyle Legault being in top form then secured a team place in the Swedish League with Dalakraft, but Mildenhall still had the first choice of his riding. A booking to ride for Edinburgh at Stoke also saw Kyle score a remarkable twenty-one points. The visit of Birmingham showed how far Mildenhall had to still go in the Premier League, and former Fen Tigers chief Graham Drury saw his Midland team inflict a defeat on Mildenhall, and led by former Tigers number one Jason Lyons.

Yet another meeting was interrupted by the rain when Mildenhall entertained Newport; this after eight heats. This was after the track was superb at the beginning of the meeting. There were also two very long delays due to crashes, and but for these the cut-off point to see the score standing at heat twelve would have been reached. This meant the re-run of this meeting would probably be on a Tuesday evening at West Row, no more vacant Saturdays or Sundays were available. Another new rider for Mildenhall was Jay Herne who stepped in for the away meeting at the Isle of Wight.

With Mildenhall suffering some injuries in an incident packed meeting against Sheffield, it was a strange line-up for the visit of Workington on 2nd September. Rider/Replacement for Tom P Madsen, Ricky Ashworth of Sheffield as guest for Kyle and Matthew Wright in at number six. However, the Tigers managed to come out on top 47-44. Then on the following Tuesday versus Newport another victory when Newport were beaten 55-38, still without Tom P and Shane Henry standing by as the number eight. The heat one time of 50.19 was a new track record and put up by Shaun Tacey. The downside however was the broken collarbone by Mark Baseby putting him out for the rest of the season. This meeting saw some programmed second half races including Kozza Smith, James Holder, Jake Knight and Shane Henry; the last two sons of former Fen Tiger legends. Other riders keen to make a start in the sport were Henning Loof and a young Australian Mitchell Davey.

Dane Jan Graveson looked impressive in some second half outings.

An interesting statistic came from the meeting with Glasgow when Paul Fry came up against Michael Cole, two of the oldest speedway riders still competing. Matthew Wright and Ricky Ashworth came to the Tigers rescue as injuries had again depleted the home squad. Kyle was the rider selected to ride in the Premier League Riders Championship at Swindon. Kyle also rode in his biggest meeting so far in the Grand Prix Challenge final at Vojens in Sweden., and a lot of Mildenhall fans flew out to cheer him on, plus a couple of riders and some backroom staff. However he was involved in a severe crash in his first ride for which he was harshly excluded; he rode on but in pain and it was found later he had sustained a broken wrist, so unfortunately his season was then over.

It was a question of who to bring into the Mildenhall team each week, now that the injury bug had really bitten hard. Rye House rider Steve Boxall and Joe Haines of Scunthorpe rode against Berwick and helped in a 54-39 win. Others were Ashworth once again at Glasgow, Josef Franc and Scott James at Berwick. Danny Betson was also drafted in as reserve guest for one meeting. A fine performance came at Berwick with a hard-fought draw. In spite of all these changes Mildenhall just done enough to reach the finals of the Young Shield, and end of season tournament for the next eight in the league, following the top four, and faced Birmingham in the quarterfinal home and away. The home leg was taken by Birmingham in a close encounter 47-43

So near and yet so far, that is how the riders and the supporters felt after the two legs of the match versus Birmingham. To go to such a top club as Birmingham and gain a superb victory was certainly a feather in the Mildenhall cap, but just two points in vain as the Brummies won it overall. Lee Complin was a great choice as a guest and he said he felt he was a real Fen Tiger and not just a guest.

One of the end of season meetings was the Shareholders Junior Trophy and among the riders were Nicky Glanz, Mark Thompson, Jerran Hart, Dan Halsey, and Shane Henry; plus Aussies James Holder and Kozza Smith with Henning Loof (Germany) and Jan Graversen from Denmark. This was run in twenty heats then a semi-final followed

-121-

by the grand final. The four battling in the final were Matt Wright, Darren Mallett, Joe Haines and Jan Gravesen and Wright took the trophy with Gravesen runner-up. A mini-match for the youngsters on 250cc bikes ended the meeting pitting Mildenhall trainees against the Dragons team, and the home line-up took the laurels.

The 2007 season wound down with the 'Big Bang' Meeting, this year four teams battled it out; Boston, Peterborough and an East Anglian team opposed Mildenhall. Top riders on view included Neils K Iversen, Leigh Lanham and Kenneth Bjerre, and it proved a fine finale as the track record was equalled in the very first heat and then Bjerre set a new record at 49'81 in heat five. For the record, the winners were the Peterborough four. A few second half heats and some Junior Grass Track demonstration races ended the night.

Of the new riders who arrived at Mildenhall at the beginning of the 2007 season Tom P Madsen had an unlucky end to the year when he was sidelined with injury, as did the top Fen Tiger Kyle Legault. Jason King was a top captain and Shawn Tacey showed much more of the form looked for from him. Jirout disappeared quickly. Jamie Smith also picked up a bad injury while Mark Thompson lost form midway through the season. Baseby, Fry and Suchanec came in and impressed.

There were two end-of-season celebrations this year, the Presentation Evening on 3rd November at the Bell Hotel in nearby Mildenhall, and fans saw their rider-of-the-year crowned. Several supporters booked in at the hotel for overnight as the evenings tended to go on quite a while. There was also the Adults and Children's Christmas Party on 2nd December at the West Row Stadium. The children's was early and followed by the grown-ups Christmas Disco, concluding with a visit from Farther Christmas.

****

2008

Once again, it was all change for the Mildenhall team after yet another hectic winter when the club ended up being owned by its supporters - the Barmy Army - led by Simon Barton and Laurence Rogers as Director of Speedway and team manager. To be known as the

Mildenhall 'Barmy Army' Fen Tigers was unique for a club to be owned more or less by its own supporters. A link with the past was Robert Henry being Training Officer. Of last years riders Kyle Legault was enticed away to Birmingham and Shaun Tacey looked like returning, but when his son decided to take to grass-track racing this was Sundays done away with so Tacey moved to a more convenient midweek track. Last years skipper Jason King decided to move north with his girl friend and linked up with Newcastle. Last seasons elder of the team, Paul Fry moved his operations to the Isle of Wight Islanders, while Tom P Madsen joined Reading, as did Tomas Suchanek

It was the Fen Tigers third season in the Premier League and the turn around of riders continued and Germany born Robbie Kessler was to be the team's captain, after being with Stoke last year and ending the year on the injured list. All the Fen Tigers were to have a 'Rider Support Team in 2008 for help them from travelling through to tyres and fuel. Youngster Mark Baseby was with the Tigers once again as he had impressed during 2007 holding his own in the Premier League although he ended the season with his feet up nursing an injury. Other newcomers were two young riders from Denmark and Grant Tregoning a New Zealand youngster that Ivan Mauger recommended to Mildenhall. He was late in arriving for the new season owing to some new regulations on his passport, which saw him waiting for a visa to be issued enabling him to travel to the United Kingdom to pursue his speedway-racing career.

The pervious season saw Jan Graversen taking some second half rides and looked to be a good signing as he came within a whisker of the Mildenhall track record in his first outing. He was joined by Casper Wortmann who also rode in a few British meetings in 2007 at various tracks, and got in touch with Mildenhall and asked for a team place and his request was granted. To cover in the early meetings for Grant the New Zealander, former Fen Tiger Shane Colvin was drafted in from his club Reading to help; he had been living in France and was looking to resume his riding which he had not done for a while. To ride at number one was the flying Finn Kij Laukkanen of whom much was expected, he being on loan from Belle Vue. Taking a reserve berth was James Cockle from nearby March, and who rode a smattering of matches with

Mildenhall last season.

To open the new campaign Rye House were the visitors to West Row in the Premier Trophy but the weather had the last word about this and after a full days practice on the Saturday, it began to rain and it poured all through the night, making the track impossible to get ready the following day. Mildenhall had started well in an Inter-League challenge at Peterborough, and although going down 56-34, things looked bright for the Premier League season. Jan Graversen top-scoring and winning two races, and Jamie Smith came into the Tigers side as a guest. The only down side was Robbie crashing out of the meeting and suffering from concussion and as a result missed a large portion of the opening meetings.

The second home meeting of the season was to see Kings Lynn as the visitors but once again, the meeting was postponed, this time it flung in a snow shower or two during the week-end. The first official match of the new season had taken place at Kings Lynn on the Wednesday night in which the Fen Tigers lost heavily by 64-24. It was also a bad night for Shane Colvin who finished up with damaged ligaments to his knee, and this after just two comeback rides; tapes exclusion and a crash; and he was out of action for the followings several weeks. So quite early on, the odds seemed to stack up against Mildenhall as they were using rider replacement for their captain and down to guest riders to cover a spate of injuries. One to commit fully to the Tigers was Kaj Laukkanen who had signed for a Polish side who were then not given a licence so he would only be missing if a Finland International meeting wanted his services. He was also due for the Grand Prix Qualifying meetings.

Throughout the seasons there were mentions of certain riders being assets of Mildenhall but not riding for them; being loaned out to other teams. Berwick's Norbert Magoski was one of these but could not ride on the Mildenhall race day of Sundays as he was riding in Poland on that day of the week. Second half racing was making a comeback as some youngsters were given the chance to impress; these including Kyle Hughes, Marc Owen and a certain Joe Jacobs and Jake Knight, son of Fen Tigers favourite Richard Knight. The length of the second half was always dependant on whether the safety fence had to come down straight after the meeting or when it could be left up over-night.

With two more midweek matches lost Mildenhall were still waiting to kick off their home meetings. However when they did manage to run at home they were embarrassed by visitors Berwick Bandits to the tune of 61-29. The visiting riders were much sharper and the Mildenhall promoters said this type of performance was unacceptable. It was guest John Oliver the Kings Lynn Australian who showed the Tigers the way as he top scored with a paid eight points. To their credit, the Fen Tigers did perk up and although again losing at home to the mighty Birmingham it was closer at 42-32. This was the position when a very bad crash in heat thirteen saw serious injury to both the Birmingham rider Phil Morris and Mildenhall's Casper Wortmann, both ending up in hospital. As with these things, some straightaway blamed the fence but the SCB Representative had passed the West Row fence as being safe and doing its job on his annual visit just a few days before the meeting

For Casper it seemed he had initially got off lightly but he took a turn for the worst and was taken to Addenbrookes Hospital at Cambridge for immediate surgery and where he was put into intensive care, but he recovered after much treatment and of course went back home to Denmark to fully recover. With some prejudicial talk about the incident the Fen Tigers stopped any photographs of the crash being circulated and did not release details of the serious aspects of the crash and injuries until after the young Dane was on the road to recovery. Another injury to contend with saw rider replacement used for Casper but the Tigers could only operate this for four weeks, and more guests were needed for cover although they were always on the lookout for a seasoned rider to come in and bolster the team. Then came more contrite rumours that captain Robbie Kessler, missing since his crash on 13th March at Peterborough was making the most of his injury by not riding, to which the management replied that this was definitely not the case and he was due to return very shortly. It seemed that when a club is struggling there are always some misguided people ready to put the boot in. A new rider did come in to Mildenhall but not the old hand as had been mooted but an exciting young seventeen-year-old Finn Jari Makinen, whom Tigers number one Kaj was to take under his wing. He was the reigning Under 21 champions back in his own country. The conditions of this signing were that after twelve outing the young Finn would be a Mildenhall asset. His debut came versus Isle of Wight when he took the place of James Cockle, and Luakkanen led from the front and posted a top score of seventeen from five rides, but in vain as the Tigers went under once again.

For the ardent Tigers supporters there were three tours involving overnight stays for this year. Two days for the Somerset Pairs and the Cardiff Grand Prix, plus the usual Scotland to Edinburgh, Berwick and Newcastle, plus another Northern trek taking in Glasgow and Workington. These were added to the trips to every away meeting if enough people booked to travel with the Fen Tigers away fans. One good thing about the Tigers trips was that those involved also got some free time to themselves and it was not all speedway and nothing else. The supporters boasted a poet in their midst who came up with an effort at times, such as
The rain and injuries won't defeat us
And you hopefully won't see our lads for dust
We hope the riders that are Finnish
Will show us their best finish

Two meetings at West Row in two days saw the Saturday night Trophy meeting gave Mildenhall a long awaited victory over the Kings Lynn Stars by the narrow margin of two points, 46-44. All supporters and riders welcomed it alike and it was fully thought the tide had turned and this was the beginning of a better run of results; but read on. It was back to the usual the next day when the Redcar Bears won by ten points at West Row in the League K O Cup 2nd leg. In the win over Kings Lynn Henning Loof was given a chance in the team and responded with a proficient performance and six well-earned points, so he was given an extended run to see what he could do. Robbie Kessler also made a return to the saddle at Redcar and scored double figures, following this up with sixteen against Kings Lynn.

Misfortune of a different variety appeared in the home meeting against Rye House when it was definitely a 'Bad Day at the Office' and the electrical problems which came about were something that could not be anticipated. After much testing as always before the meeting gets underway, the gremlins crept in as the start gate was shorting out the whole system. After putting Mark Baseby's father to work; he was an electrician, the tapes were mended but with no starting lights, this eventually being overcome with an extra switch coming into operation. The delays had begun before the meeting when two alcohol tests of two riders were shown as failures by the referee. Nevertheless, but after some consultation they were re-tested much further away from the pit area which gave off a lot of methanol fumes the two riders were given the thumbs up. On top of all this there were long intervals when there were fallers and re-runs, plus some tape exclusions. Once again the Tigers poet laureate came up with.

"Let's raise a prayer that this week we find; no gremlins at West Row, And we can get all equipment working, And can get on with the show."

There were no such delays and stoppages the next meeting at West Row; in fact, there was nothing happening at all when the rains once again stopped all action and the meeting was put off in the morning to save a lot of travelling to find the match postponed. Mildenhall were ready to give their new signing his first outing Michal Rajkowski. Finally, New Zealander Grant Tregoning was in the country but not with Mildenhall as they had loaned him out to Buxton Hitmen to give him some much-wanted rides to bring him up to speed. Watched by Laurence Rogers he made his debut versus Boston and put up a creditable score of six, following this with thirteen at Scunthorpe, where several Fen Tiger fans made the journey to watch the young Kiwi in action. However, there was another rider signed by the Fen Tigers in Michal Rajkowski who took on the number one race colours.

The home meeting with Edinburgh Monarchs saw another defeat and it showed that for the visitors their two reserve riders amassed a paid twenty-eight points while the two Fen Tigers at six and seven totalled just five between them. Up to this stage of the season, Mildenhall had not fielded a team of all Fen Tigers riders, but it was getting close and when Mark Baseby came back from injury this feat could well be on the cards and perhaps the tide will turn. Guests were the order of the day up to now and included Lee Smart, Barry Evans, Chris Schramm, Kyle Hughes, and Jack Roberts, the best show coming from Hughes. Just as the team were beginning to look a mite more settled Jan Graversen picked up an injury, but with a minimum of three weeks out of action being quoted he was back on the bike very quickly against Somerset Rebels.. Kaj Laukkanen also revealed he had been riding in discomfort for the past few meetings as he had suffered a damaged shoulder, which was slow to heal.

For the first time this season Mildenhall fielded a team consisting of all their own riders; no guests, but on a wet and heavy track versus Newcastle Diamonds gating from the Tigers was not up to standard and with passing down to a minimum Newcastle took the points. When it started to rain during the racing the referee was asked for a short delay while Huggy got to work on the track to try to improve matters, but the man in charge wanted to proceed as quickly as possible and get the meeting finished. It was soon noticed that the attendance was slowly getting smaller and way down on the number through the turnstiles to break even. To try to boost the crowd numbers ten thousand brochures were printed and distributed to the Tourist Board, hotels, public houses and any other outlet they could come up with. On the rider front the Mildenhall management were trying to get better riders in as some of the present seven did not seem to relish some of the meetings.

Going into the home encounter with a patched-up Redcar side the Fen Tigers were expected to have a chance to pick up their first Premier League win of the season. However it turned into a disaster when the Tigers were comprehensively beaten 58-35. All seven riders and team manager attended an after-the-meeting fans forum where all kinds of questions were asked, most accepting they had put on a below par performance. The team had been given a dressing down by Laurence after heat five and told to pull their socks up in no uncertain terms, but this did not seem to work, some fans seemed to blame the team manager for the desperate situation. It could be said that things were not just working out now and it seemed that some changes in personnel was on the cards. On the back of some feeble showings, the Fen Tigers had missed qualifying for the Premier Best Pairs Championship.

To further upset the team building Robbie Kessler was missing from two matches when he picked up a chest infection and then Jari Makinen faced six weeks at least after dislocating his ankle and breaking a bone in his foot as well and faced some surgery back in his home country to repair the injury. Tomas Suchanek guested for Jari and as always was a popular rider at West Row putting up a double figure score that included two heat wins against Scunthorpe. After heat four, the track staff went out to do a major re-grading of the racing circuit. With the visitors riding hard for points there were some incidents and the referee had to come down from the box to calm the situation in the pits at one time. The Scunthorpe promotion had a lot to say which the Tigers took exception to.

After Henning Loof had struggled for some time, it was decided to bring in Matt Wright at number seven, and when Kaj Laukkanen was needed for Finland in the World Team Cup in Slovenia, Mildenhall asset Chris Schramm came in as a guest replacement versus Glasgow Tigers. A rider the Fen Tigers wanted to bring in was the worst kept secret as they battled to sign Dutchman Theo Pijper who was heavily engaged on the continent. Mildenhall were ready to send a van to France to pick up his bikes in readiness for a West Row debut, and a car to pick Theo up at the airport. However, this failed to happen and another week went past.

The chains of Mildenhall riders decided to break in the Glasgow meeting which didn't improve matters, and when Kaj contacted the Fen Tigers he said he had urgent family matters to sort out in his home country and Mildenhall were granted twenty-eight days leave to bring in guest riders to re-place the Flying Finn. He said he wanted to be back at Mildenhall but needed the time off, so the Tigers were set a task to seek out a re-placement for him probably in the long run. It does not rain but it pours with Kessler still missing because of his illness, and Mildenhall were having talks with him as to when he was planning to resume riding. On the other hand, Theo Pijper finally arrived to take his place in the team at the beginning of July. He had ridden for Edinburgh and Berwick in 2007.

While all this was going on the Supporters Club were all doing their bit to help matters along and especially on the cash side of things. A Race-Night was run at the Stadium which proved popular and raised a healthy sum and a new event planned was a book sale in the main bar

(17) A rare action shot with STEFAN NIELSEN behind

(18 top JASON GARRITY
(18 bottom) LEWIS BLACKBIRD

(19 top) LEWIS BLACKBIRD & CAMERON HEEPS the National
League Pairs champions 2012
(19 bottom) MILDENHALL 2012 with mascot and promotion staff

(20 top) JOE JACOBS
(20 bottom) CAMERON HEEPS

when all fans were asked to de-clutter their homes and donate any kind of books, not just speedway and sport, were gratefully accepted. This brought another tidy sum for the coffers.

After a rained-off home meeting and two more away trips resulting in heavy defeats it came to the attention that a record was on the way that nobody wanted as Mildenhall were fighting not just for survival but having not won a league meeting so far this season. The horrifying truth that they could go through the season losing every match was very much on the cards. As the band of loyal supporters was also getting smaller each week, many of these hoping to be there when the Fen Tigers broke their 2008 duck, money coming through the gate was being reduced each meeting.

Desperate for riders in came Marek Mroz a former Newport rider who drove over from Poland to join the Fen Tigers as soon as he could, and a fresh number one in Sebastian Ruminski the twenty-eight-year-old Polish rider who dropped everything and rushed to the Fen Tigers aid, making his debut at Kings Lynn. He had previously been with Berwick and Newport. Pijper was having a bundle of trouble with his own bikes and it was not known when he would be able to return to West Tow to take his place in the team. But to counter this Mikal Rajkowski then picked up an injured ankle and had to go back to his home country to get the specialist treatment for this. All this going on did not stop the loyal band of away supporters who had already booked places for the three match trip to Scotland; in fact there were to be two coaches conveying them north of the border. Also with more riders from abroad coming to Mildenhall some supporters were offering these a place to stay in England when needed; those were the fans every team would like to have supporting them. To try to secure the future of the Fen Tigers talks were already happening with the stadium landlord Allen Trump, with negotiations going well as to how the speedway will operate the next season.

The trip to Scotland was a much harder one this season with all the talk of whether the Fen Tigers would complete the season and the weekly struggle to recruit riders to fill the ever opening spaces in the team. Result wise was not any batter when all three meeting saw defeats;

69-21 at Edinburgh, 72-18 at Berwick and ending at Newcastle on the wrong end of a 68-22 scoreline. However, the Fen Tiger riders came out after each meeting to thank their travelling supporters for showing the Mildenhall colours. On the subject of riders, young Ben Hopwood answered a late call to travel to Berwick as the Mildenhall number eight, and ended up by being given three rides for his efforts. Luke Priest also said yes when approached and drove to Newcastle to take a place in the line-up. Special thanks were given by the Mildenhall promotion to Adam McKinna who stepped into the Tigers team on the Saturday and Sunday and welcomed a chance by trying so hard he blew his engine in his efforts. Yet another name was added to the Mildenhall list as Lee Smart joined the Suffolk outfit after being suddenly released by Birmingham. His addition meant Matt Wright went out on loan to Weymouth, while an approach to Stoke for the services of Barrie Evans was stalled when they had slapped a twenty-eight day ban for him withholding his services. Nevertheless, he eventually appeared in the team for the home meeting with Rye House when Casper Wortmann made a surprising return to the fold after his serious injuries early in the season. He had telephoned the club and pronounced himself fit to ride again.

With money at an all time low and to aid the take-over by Allen Trump, appeals did not bring in the extra cash needed. Nevertheless, just when it seemed the Fen Tigers were going out of business once again, in stepped the Kings Lyn duo of Keith and Jonathan Chapman, father and son, to be the new promotion team This was after being approached by Simon Barton who made every effort to keep the Mildenhall club afloat after the Trump deal fell through. The new promoters had bought the assets of the club and the licence but this did not include owning the track. The first call this new promotion made was to Paul Lee to get him riding for Mildenhall once again, and straight away he agreed as he said he always loved being at Mildenhall., and Henning Loof came back into the line-up as well. There were six meeting until the end of the season and the first meeting for this company was versus Reading on 31st August, and this saw an increase in the attendance straight away; but were they wanting to see how the new boys ran the meeting or did they really supported the Fen Tigers. No one worried about this as cash on the turnstiles meant a little leeway for

-131-

the future. One departure was that of team manager Laurence Rogers who had been doing a difficult job as best he could, and in his place came ex Mildenhall favourite Richard Knight, at least until the end of the season. Simon Barton did not leave but took on another role in promoting the club and community work. Simon had been supporting the club for well over thirty years. Amongst other riders brought in to make up the team on several occasions were Ario Bugeja of Redcar, Jay Herne and Andrew Bargh. This was to no avail and Mildenhall ended a season to rub from the memory of finishing rock bottom of the Premier League and losing all the matches; a record nobody wants or are proud of

****

2009

After the disastrous campaign of 2008 in the Premier League Mildenhall decided this was not for them and joined the newly former National League, the new third tier of Speedway in Britain. It had been a hectic winter for the club and it seemed at one time that the Fen Tigers were down and out. However, long time supporter and member of the track staff Ray Maskall sat down with colleagues, and a business plan was set up with Ray as Chairman, to form Fen Speed 09. Then they attracted the sponsorship from Funky Catering, a food firm based in Cambridge. An application to rent the stadium from Dave Coventry was agreed and Mildenhall were on their way once again.

Then the formation of a team was sorted out, and the first to put pen to paper was Barrie Evans who had returned to the Fen Tigers towards the end of the previous season. Then in came two young riders Oliver Rayson and Joe Jacobs, from Bury St Edmunds and Ipswich respectively. This carried the Mildenhall tradition of bringing youngsters to the sport into the new season. Sixteen-year-old Rayson had spent his first season with Boston and was a bright prospect, while Jacobs was a junior from Ipswich Witches and the youngest rider in the Tigers colours. Not such a new face was Mark Thompson coming back to his roots once again followed by the very experienced David Mason who had just taken a year off from the sport and was looking for a return, and was the team's captain. Australian Leigh Boujos was looking to come to the country and to the Fen Tigers but once again experiencing difficulties with a visa meant Dean Felton and Gary

Cottham - ex Rye House and Sittingbourne - made up the rest of the new-found team.

The fresh National League was made up of ten clubs including the brand new Bournemouth Bucaneers who rode at Poole, and virtually a second team of that town's Elite League side, and the revived Newport. Sittingbourne had decided that league racing was not for them although the track was still operating as a training facility as it had done for many years now. Isle of Wight, like the Fen Tigers, also dropped down to the National League after struggling in the Premier League. There could not have been a more hectic beginning to a season than this tear when the Fen Tigers started with four meetings in four days.

What a match to start the fresh Mildenhall era than a visit from nearby Kings Lynn Barracudas in the National League Knock-out Cup. Meetings between the Barracudas, then as Boston, and the Fen Tigers have been on the agenda ever since Mildenhall were formed back in the seventies, and it was still Boston under the new guise as they were now operating out of Saddlebow Road. They included a rider who had assisted the Tigers in Scott Campos. Jake Knight the son of Richard Knight, had also been given a chance to obtain a spot in the team. The match ended level at 46 points each with Jamie Smith top scoring with seventeen as the visitors moved into the next round having won by sixteen points in the home leg. However, Mildenhall had started in brilliant form and were victors at Rye House in the first League meeting 52-41 as Barrie Evans piled up a maximum.

The Easter week-end proved a great starting point for the new Fen Tigers as the opening meeting at West Row drew one of the largest crowds for some time and the feel-good factor was back again in the supporters hearts, and the dark days of the previous season was really done away with. New team manager John Adams was said to be over-the-moon with the team over the first few matches and said it looked well for the future of Mildenhall Speedway. The sizeable crowd turned up once again for the second league match versus the Isle of Wight and witnessed a Mildenhall victory 55-37 as all the home riders chalked up a heat win or a paid win. The second half saw long-term rider Dean Garrod having an outing after being out of the sport for a while. There was several times this year when the two sports clashed on the weekend. The track workers had been caught out the previous week when the weather forecast said rain in the afternoon so the track was not watered, but no rain came and the track soon turned very slick and not the best surface for racing, so the BBC was blamed for this happening.

Rye House Cobras were next up at West Row when the start time was put back to six o'clock to give the track staff extra time to prepare after the stockcar meeting on Saturday night. The win by 59-31 saw the Fen Tigers complete the double over their long-term rivals, as two tactical rides by the visitors saw the rider nominated finishing last each time. Once again, all the Mildenhall riders had a heat win or paid win. There was also an Academy match in the second half where the Mildenhall riders were Nick Lawrence, Adam Kirby and Tom Stokes. It was a not so good day the following week against for although the Tigers won 49-40 over Kings Lynn Barracudas the meeting was somewhat marred by injuries to both the Smith brothers, Jamie and Darren both sustaining bad injuries; they were on opposite sides in the meeting. For this match Mildenhall had re-arranged their line-up with Cottham out of the side as was Mark Thompson and in came Darren Smith and Luke Priest who had started the season at Bournemouth.

Just when it was thought that Mildenhall were on the up after some team alterations they tasted defeat at Buxton. Also the following Sunday at West Row when Newport registered an away victory, and in doing so provided the race winner in thirteen of the heats, the Tigers two heat winner being Luke Priest and David Mason; a very sorry performance. There had been a three-week interruption when wet weather resulted in no racing at home. The all-conquering Bournemouth Buccaneers were next and despite unearthing a new Australian start in Dakota North, who top scored from the reserve berth for Mildenhall, the visitors won 48-42. Dakota followed this up with another double figure (13+1) in the next match, but could not save the Fen Tigers slipping to their fifth loss in a row; Buxton took the lead in heat three and were never pulled back although it went to a last heat decider. The seventeen-year-old Victorian was the son of former Stoke rider Rod North. He had been in England two years previous after winning the Australian Under sixteen's championship, and had a few tentative rides. It was yet another Sunday of woe the next time out when Scunthorpe Saints took the league points at West Row 49-43

Two Under 21 'Test' matches saw the Youthful British stars ride against the young Australian riders at Weymouth and then Kings Lynn and the Tigers interest in these was the inclusion of their new rider Dakota North who showed up well in both meetings. However he picked up an injury which then kept him out of the Mildenhall side for a while, which gave reserve Nick Laurence an outing in the Tigers colours. Back at West Row the Mildenhall run of defeats was halted but by only a draw at home to the Plymouth Devils at forty-five points each, this being down to a maximum 5-1 from Evans and Priest in the last heat. The next three away meeting saw the Tigers win at Kings Lynn but lost two more on the road.

With the two elder statesmen of the side, Mason and Felton not scoring the regular number of points expected they left the Mildenhall team, Mason took up with Rye House and Felton joined Isle of Wight. In came Jamie Burkinshaw and another Aussie sensation in Taylor Poole who started with two wins and a second in the Mildenhall victory over the Weymouth Wildcats 57-35. This new Aussie was the son of former Peterborough favourite Mick Poole, and has taken over from North who headed home to recover from his injuries. Seventeen-year-old Poole hailed from New South Wales, rode for the Central Coast Club, and had appeared for the Australian side in the Youth World Cup. Birkinshaw top-scored with four wins in his Tigers debut. All the home riders took at least one heat win with Barrie Evans taking over the captaincy. This home victory was the Tigers first since 31 May, and they had been reeling from the long run of losses at West Row.

It was back to a home defeat next time out when Buxton once again escaped with the points in a meeting which was only remarkable for Mildenhall when Taylor Poole started heat fourteen back 15 metres for a tape offence, only to storm through the field to come home first, a great ride. The Tigers were also not helped in this encounter when Evans engine gave up the ghost in heat ten leaving him at the tapes. After some disappointing performances at home, Mildenhall surprised many with a victory at High Edge over the Buxton Hitmen with a clear all-round team effort this coming after losing at home twice against the Derbyshire team. A more than welcome home win came over Weymouth as Taylor Poole and Barrie Evans led the way with a paid eighteen from Reserve by the young Aussie and a five-ride maximum from the captain. The only down side was Birkinshaw feeling decidedly unwell and withdrew from the meeting after winning heat four. Luke Priest and Barrie Evans were the Fen Tigers in the National League Pairs and showed up well early on but the winners turned out to be Newport Hornets. The National League Riders Championship saw Evans the Tigers representative, who was way down the field at the end; he had won this title in 2003. Rayson and Jacobs were the two riders in the GB Under 18 championships at Scunthorpe, but after both started well they faded in the end.

Mildenhall finished off the season with three home meetings and winning all three to send the supporters into the winter break hoping the tide will turn the following summer. However, an individual meeting rounded off the 2009 campaign, or to give its full title the Renaissance Property Management Shareholders Trophy. As well as the Tigers riders, the field included Simon Lambert, Darren Mallett and Jari Makinen in the sixteen-rider field. A run-off at the end made Mallett the victor with Mildenhall's Taylor Poole in third place. The meeting also saw some lovely old speedway bikes on display and having a short series of races, their elderly riders sporting the old colours of Norwich Stars, Liverpool Pirates, Odsal Tudors and Cradley Heath.

****

2010
The new season started with a challenge match against the Team Vikings but the rain put paid to that meeting and the season finally got under way with the British Under 21's semi-final at West Row, and the victor was Scott Campos, a former Tiger but then with Kings Lynn Young Stars. A bizarre set of events meant this meeting was late in getting under way, as the ambulance on the way to the track was held up and then helped out at an accident, meaning the West Row crowd had to wait awhile as the racing started later than usual. It was at the end of April that the Mildenhall National League season got underway with a visit from Kings Lynn Young Stars, although the away fixtures had

-136-

begun the night before at Rye House Cobra's where they really put it across the Fen Tigers on a night to forget, registering a 60-31 win. The Fen Tigers were also riding under a new sponsor with 'Art & Stitch of Peterborough coming in.

Mildenhall paraded a new number one in the shape of Jerran Hart the Ipswich born rider, who was with Bournemouth in 2009 with the rest of the line-up having been at West Row the season before. Missing too were Birkinshaw and Taylor Poole, the latter opting to join Ipswich in a league higher. The Kings Lynn meeting got off to a bad start for the Tigers with a 5-1 reverse in the first heat and as early as heat six Hart had to don the black and white for a tactical ride, which he duly won. However, at the end the visitors were the victors 50-43. The best of the Tigers was newcomer Hart who took the chequered flag three times in his total of 14 points, the rest of the team only managing three wins between them.

Six days later Mildenhall had the quick chance to avenge this loss when they were at the Norfolk Arena and this time recorded their first win of the year. Jerran Hart led this, Barrie Evans with three wins each, and the local boys Jacobs and Rayson with two win each to their name. One down side was losing Matt Bates in his first ride. Unfortunately, the following day the visit to Buxton was a disappointment, going down 58-37 in the first leg of the Knock out Cup. The Hitmen were next up at West Row in the second leg when both sides had their number one unavailable due to other commitments. Darren Mallett was the Tigers guest rider who proceeding to top score with thirteen points but the visitors reserve pair put up twenty-nine points between them. Mildenhall lost interest in the competition with a 50-40 home defeat, and the home team could only manage four heat wins, a dismal performance.

The Supporters Club was soon arranging events and different ways to raise cash for the team, and a chance to have a photograph with a favourite rider amongst its rewards. A special offer to help with the Riders Equipment Fund was also on the cards and a special jar was available to drop any spare money into each meeting for the benefit of the Academy team. The Shale-Shifters competition was then inviting all and sundry to buy a spot on the terraces at twenty-five pounds for the

-137

season, a draw being made from these each meeting for a prize of two complimentary tickets for the home meetings. On top of all this was still the meeting raffle with proceeds going from this to the rider's fuel at home and away. For all this it meant the supporters always felt they were all members of the same team; all Fen Tigers.

Dudley Heathens away was always going to be a tough assignment but the Fen Tigers puller off a great win to possibly kick start their season 46-44 with Hart, Jacobs and Evans all in double figures. This was the last meeting for Matt Bates who found the travelling from Exeter too much and swopped clubs with Matt Wright at Plymouth, who linked up with Mildenhall for the fourth time from his home at nearby Harlow. Then with ten heat wins the Tigers were the victors over Rye House Cobra's 48-32 as Joe Jacobs was the top man with a paid seventeen from number seven. This win was overshadowed however by the passing of Jean Mascall the wife of the Mildenhall chairman Ray, and suitable expressions were recorded by a minutes of applause and flowers placed on the spot where she loved to stand to watch her beloved Tigers. Ray met Jean at the Mildenhall Speedway and had been keen supporters from then onwards. Ray then decided to stand down as the Mildenhall chairman after a few more meetings, but still kept involved in a smaller but important way. Team Manager John Adams would then take charge and a potential buyer for the club was to be sought.

It was a quick return to West Row for Bates as he was in the Plymouth Devils line-up at Mildenhall, and what was thought to be a tough meeting ended 60-33 in the Tigers favour. Then they made it four wins on the trot with victory over the Weymouth Wildcats. The new averages came out for this fixture and Joe Jacobs moved up into the team proper, and another away success was put under their belt by winning at the Isle of Wight, not a good place normally for the visitors. A prestige even was held at West Row with the BSPA National League Four Team Championship Finals, eight teams being involved in two groups of four, the top two progressing to the final stages. Twelve of the riders had been or were Fen Tigers riders. The National League co-ordinator Peter Morrish was present to present the trophy to the winners but the meeting was washed out by a thunderstorm and abandoned after

-138-

twelve heats with Mildenhall leading their group by quite a margin.

A loss down in Wales to Newport was followed by a fine win over Bournemouth Buccaneers the reigning champions of the League 53-37. This victory was down to the minor placings as the visitors had ten last places to Mildenhall's five. Seven wins out of the last eight matches put the Fen Tigers into second place in the National League table and a spot in the ply-offs was on the cards, which they consolidated with victory over Isle of Wight, Jon Armstrong making a return to the Mildenhall colours as a guest number one. He was beaten just once in the meeting to share memories of not so long ago. With three weeks until the next meeting, it came as a shock to everyone that Mildenhall were closing down if no buyer could be found to carry on the club. The League helped in every way by giving the Tigers more time to seek ways of continuing and even thought of keeping the racing going with some away meetings. However, this was all in vain and the Fen Tigers dropped out of the National League; sad because they were in a great position to take some trophies this season.

****

2011

After having to come to an end halfway through the 2010 season when the attendances dipped too low and the promotion had no option than to suspend operations. A comeback was always on the cards this time however. The BPA tried unsuccessfully for several weeks in the summer of 2010 to keep the Fen Tigers afloat but they were unable to do so. Undeterred the Mildenhall supporters soon got together and formed the 'Secure Mildenhall Speedway' (SMS) and worked hard through the winter to raise money and support for the Fen Tigers ready for the re-birth. They carried on when the new season started and together with the Supporters Club are going great with raising much needed cash along the way. Their first big effort was a Buffet and Race Night at the prodigious Worlington Hall. Coach trip to away meetings was also on the agenda once again, as the Fen Tigers had proved many times before to be the best supported team for many miles.

When at first a promotion team was put together and put before the National League to compete in 2011, they refused to accept Mildenhall into the league, although they had all the right things in place. It seemed it was a clash between one of the new promoters and the league officials, and when another group consisting of Chris Louis, Michael Lee and Kevin Jolly with Robert Henry earmarked for team manager, the National League done a u-turn and the Fen Tigers were up and running once more. The promotion were all either ex Tiger riders or local East Anglian riders of some note with Kevin Jolly as chairman and Robert Henry as Team Manager.

Although quite late in the close season, the riders were soon being brought in. First was the number one and the new Mildenhall captain 24 year-old James Brundle who had been a rider when the Tigers were in the Premier League, but had since done most of his riding with Kings Lynn. He had a year in the Elite League with Eastbourne in 2008, had a year out the following campaign, when he was mechanic for Troy Batchelor, then returned at Kings Lynn in 2010, coupled with spell at Bournemouth. He was also an England Under 21 rider his debut being versus Sweden at Wolverhampton in 2003. Then it was announced that the two youngsters Joe Jacobs and Oliver Rayson who had been in the team the year before were coming back, Joe being a protégé of former England rider Jeremy Doncaster and had ended in fourth place in the 2008 British Under 15 Championship. When Mildenhall closed in 2010, he rode for Rye House where he finished runner-up in the British Under 18 Championship.

Next in was Aaron Baseby, aged twenty the younger of the brothers who had started on their careers at Sittingbourne in Division Three. He had made his first appearance for the Kent side against Stoke in 2005 with one ride producing no points. He had spent 2009 with Bournemouth. Jack Hargreaves was next to sign, he had taken a time out of the sport but decided he was ready for a return with the Fen Tigers when they came calling. He had started out at Stoke in 2004 in both the Conference and Premier League sides, then 2006 saw him at Redcar and Stoke once more the following season; ending back at Redcar halfway through the season, with a spell at Birmingham.

Nevertheless it was then rather surprising when it was made known that Oliver Rayson had been transferred to Kings Lynn while in return

Lewis Blackbird made the opposite journey, as he always said that he wanted to join Mildenhall, as his father had been a star rider for them some years back. At Sittingbourne for 2006 and Oxford 2007, he was not seen in speedway until returning in late 2010. A former Rye House rider in Daniel Halsey was next to put pen to paper, he had started out with Rye House in 2005 staying until 2009 before having some rides in the Premier League with Birmingham. He then joined Bournemouth and ended the year with Weymouth. The top signing came with young 15 year-old Australian Cameron Heeps from Perth a young champion back in Western Australia, and who would feature at reserve and a lot was expected of this young Aussie. His partner at Reserve was to be Danny Stoneman with Plymouth in 2009 and Weymouth in 1010.

Problems started for the new promotion team when a visa for the young Cameron Heaps was proving very hard to obtain and it seemed that time was against them but they promised to work hard at this and bring the youngster to West Row as soon as possible. The top two riders with just under nine averages were Brundle and Jack Hargreaves and the team nearly picked itself for the first round of meetings. However after just one meeting Danny Stoneman decided it was a too long a journey to Mildenhall from his West Country base each Sunday, so in came Nick Laurence a reserve rider from 2010 who had had fourteen rides as Mildenhall number eight in 2009, and who had just begun to settle down when the team folded. The four-man-team promotion also promised to return to the special dates for young riders to come to West Row and start their careers with some expert coaching from the top ex-Tigers riders, and this could well unearth a star as the Academy had done in the past.   The first of these special days saw a substantial crowd of youngsters come along to test out their ability.

It was straight into competitive action for the first meeting at West Row when Dudley Heathens came to call; they had been made favourites to be top dogs in the National League, even before a lap had been raced. The Fen Tigers re-launch was declared a resounding success The fans turned up in their hundreds for this opening meeting showing that speedway was always going to be part of the Mildenhall scene, probably the biggest crowd for a few years; eight hundred programmes had been ordered for the meeting but quickly sold out. It was also a chance to get together some of the old-timers for a re-union, and amongst those who showed up were Mel Taylor, Barry Klatt, Trevor Jones, Mick Hines, Mike Spink and Ray Bales.

The crowd were treated to a special meeting of thrills and spills before the Fen Tigers won by just one point 45-44 The Tigers taking the lead in the last heat. The first heat of a new era saw the new captain James Brundle take the chequered flag followed by young Aaron Baseby, they were ahead of former Tigers favourite Barrie Evans. Brundle had an up and down meeting as his two wins and a second place saw him beaten by another ex Mildenhall rider Adam Roynon, and an engine failure, but finished in style in heat fifteen from the unfavoured outside gate to beat Roynon, who had set up a new track record earlier of 49.8. The opening meeting also saw a return of the man in the white coat, announcer Kevin Long, sadly missed the previous season, but back to charm as all once again.

Three nights later the trip to Kings Lynn Starlets saw Mildenhall come away with a well-earned draw of forty-five points each; a great performance and a cracking start for the new Tigers. This meeting saw a substantial attendance of Tigers fans making the trip to cheer on their favourites. Came the first weekend in May and another new team was seen at West Row in the shape of Belle Vue Colts with their legendary Aces body colours. There was an unusual first heat when young Baseby fell but remounted but was unlucky to be lapped and of course excluded, and as the Belle Vue number two had fell it became a 3-2 advantage to the visitors. There were six falls in the first five heats as the track was catching both sets of riders out by being quite deep and lost of drive was being picked up at the wrong moments. Some people were pointing to the Saturday night Stock Cars for the track conditions once again. A fall by Daniel Halsey handed the visitors a big advantage and they went ahead. Both sides had their moments before the Tigers came out on top to get just two points for a very close encounter. Brundle (12 +1), Hargreaves (13+1) and Lewis Blackbird ((10) were top scorers. The return visit to Manchester was not as good for the Tigers as they slipped to a 59-32 defeat

Local rivals Kings Lynn Young Stars were next at West Row with a team containing three past Tigers riders and Jake Knight son of Tigers past favourite Richard Knight. Ashley Birks came in as a guest for Lynn. Once again, the riders struggled with the track early on but after an n even first half the Fen Tigers soared, away to win handsomely 56-37 for their first three points haul of the season. Captain James Brundle rode to a 12-point maximum with Lewis Blackbird and Joe Jacobs joining him in double figures. Off the track and into the local community were James Brundle and Lewis Blackbird who went along to help open Wilkinson's new shop in Mildenhall, and who presented to the Fen Tigers a £250 cheque to use for the Mildenhall Speedway Academy. The Mildenhall Supporters Club now re-emerged joined by the 'Secure Mildenhall Speedway' (SMS) group to be all under the same banner.

Again, the Tigers disappointed on their travels and met with a 57-36 loss at Stoke, but hey they were still going great guns and the first away win cannot be far away. The Isle of Wight were next at West Row and after a bad tumble by their young reserve John Resch which saw him off the hospital with a broken leg the meeting went the Mildenhall way and a big victory by 61-33. After a slow start to the season, Joe Jacobs scorched to a paid maximum, just when he was down the order at reserve that seem to suit him just at the right time. Lewis Blackbird moved up in the team order and still performing well. The team were flying but came down to earth when the next night the away meeting at Newport was rained-off.

Came June and the home leg of the League KO Cup 1st leg versus newly resurrected Hackney Hawks, led by ex Mildenhall favourite Barrie Evans, and again two more Fen Tigers in their team. Again, they lost a reserve rider Shane Hazelden, injured in the second heat and it showed as he had been flying for the Hawks so far this season. Mildenhall took real advantage and reduced the Hawks to just two race winners, and roared to a first leg win of 60-32, a lead of twenty-eight to take to the second leg. Captain Brundle was missing with a knee injury and the Tigers operated rider-replacement while Jack Hargreaves took over as captain, and Shane Henry stood by at number eight. This meeting saw Aaron Baseby come into his own with a score of 14 +3 which included three heat victories; Blackbird and Joe Jacobs weighed in with 13 and 15 respectively. Cameron Heeps had now arrived on British shores and met with another setback as he was not allowed to ride by the British SPA for some reason, but he showed what he could do with a sparkling four laps after the Hackney meeting, leaving the supporters to applaud his efforts.

It was bad luck for Nick Lawrence when he was dropped from the team after some very poor scores and for the meeting at Rye House young Academy rider Adam Portwood was given his chance. The second leg at Rye House where Hackney were riding their meetings saw the Fen Tigers gain their first away win of the season buy completely blowing away the opposition. They were to meet the Isle of Wight in the semi-final. Cameron Heaps was again with the Mildenhall team and had three second half rides winning two in as fast time as the match times and showing what he could add to the Tigers line-up. Having some training rides before the home meetings began was nine-year-old Lewis Whitmore who was competing in the British Under 15 (125 class) for the 2011 season.

After some impressive performances for Mildenhall, Rye House took on James Brundle for their Premier League team, signing full-time for them so the Tigers had to bring in another rider to the side. This turned out to be Mark Baseby the older of the two brothers. He had watched Aaron show his good form in the Tigers colours and quickly joined up with Mildenhall once again.

The Mildenhall pair in National League Pairs at Newport were Hargreaves and Blackbird who progressed from second in their group and only narrowly missed out the grand final. With only a small selection of clubs making up the National League this year some long breaks were occurring and it was after a three-week interruption Mildenhall next welcomed the Buxton Hitmen to West Row. They were the reigning League Champions and who once again included three ex Mildenhall riders in their team. For the Fen Tigers it started badly when Jack Hargreaves crashed out in heat one and took no further part in the meeting. However the rest of the team pulled their weight and came out on top 47-43, the two reserves Heeps and Jacobs both ringing up twelve points as top scorers. The visit to Buxton provided Mildenhall with one point as they lost by the narrowest of margins 45-44, on a night when track conditions were not at their best, and the lead changed hands a few times.

It was then the weather decided to take a hand in the speedway world and the home leg of the Knock Out Cup semi-final against the Isle of Wight was rained off. Then again, when the Tigers journeyed to the Isle of Wight for what would have been the second leg, this was abandoned after just six heats completed with the Tigers 21-9 in front. They had reeled off five wins from six heats when the rains came with a vengeance and a halt was called. The home meeting versus Hackney was the next up and the first for a month, and with the team places juggled round Captain Lewis Blackbird rode an immaculate fifteen-point maximum as the Tigers triumphed 57-35. The visitors Ben Morley had an eventful time ending as the Hackney top scorer but crashing straight through the safety fence on the second bend, but fortunately walking away. His tactical ride in heat nine gave him maximum points as his partner was excluded for 'not making a genuine attempt to race', this after he showed almost to a halt yards from the tapes to allow Morley past for the win. It is not many times this rule is implemented. Hackney did not think much of this decision and they were said to be putting in a complaint about the referee.

On the individual riders front Joe Jacobs was called into the Great Britain squad for the European Under-19 semi-final in Sweden, and this was great to see a Mildenhall rider in a GB squad, and a reward for him after a slow start to the season. Joe also took part in the British Under-19 Championship at Rye House but a couple of third places cost him and he ended in seventh spot. Jack Hargreaves had taken over as Mildenhall's captain and was revelling in the post and taking his post of responsibility, this being a great appointment by the promotional team.

Two away meetings provided the Fen Tigers with five vital points, four of them at title hunting Dudley with one of the best performances of the season, led by Cameron Heeps with twenty points in a 51-38 victory. This was one of the most fiercely contested meetings of the summer as the Tigers held the lead throughout, but there was controversy in heat nine when Lewis Blackbird was excluded for taking out Ashley Morris on the first bend to let Dudley claim a 5-1 to reduce the margin to just five points. Nevertheless, the visitors ended by extending their lead to thirteen points in a win that stunned the rest of the National League teams. Then after being ten points in the lead at Newport, they ended losing by a singles point 47-46 but came away with another point towards the play-off places in the League. Daniel Halsey was the top Tiger in this visit to Wales. One of the toughest home fixtures was with Stoke who were then in third position in the league, and led by the Tigers fans favourite (?) rider Simon Lambert who totalled twenty-one of his teams 43 points could not save them from a 49-43 defeat. In this meeting, a team from the past re-appeared when for the first time in twenty years Milton Keynes Knights returned to the speedway world. This came in a second half match against the Mildenhall Academy. For the home side it was great to see Trevor Heath back in action and with four straight wins. MK had more fixtures planned and were looking for a site for a new track.

An away point came from a 45-45 draw at the Isle of Wight, but unfortunately they also arrived back home with a wrist injury for Cameron, which sidelined him for some meetings. Ben Morley came in as a guest versus Scunthorpe Saints as the Tigers battled to a 47-43 win, and in the visiting team was a young rider, name of Stefan Nielsen, registering three points. Dan Halsey provided some drama as he picked off the two visiting riders in heat fourteen after a bad start, to take a 5-1. Neilsen slammed into the fence with his bike collecting team-mate Worrell when it spun across the track. It was at this meeting that Ivan Mauger MBE OBE was at West Row signing copies of his new book. Many things went on at the stadium each meeting; 'meet the riders' and for the children 'face painting' most ending with the markings of a tiger. Another extensive project was raising funds for an air fence that was beginning to get underway. The annual Stoke meeting saw Mildenhall end up in fourth place in the National League Fours. With three meeting to go Mildenhall were in second place with a 100% home record.

The semi-final of the League KO Cup versus Isle of Wight finally was run and Mildenhall got a sizable twenty-point lead to defend in the second-leg. Guest for the Tigers this time was Jamie Pickard who weighed in with five points in a match where every Tigers rider had at least one heat win. After the stock car racing the night before which left the track in a mess the track staff led by Bob Ellis did a magnificent job to get it ready for the speedway the next day. This was the middle fixture in a very busy weekend that started with a win at Hackney, ending with rather sizeable defeat at Scunthorpe where things did not go so well. Nikki Lee was to the front in the effort to raise the necessary funds towards the air fence, and due to five sponsors with one thousand pounds each coming in the idea was nearly there, ten thousand pounds was the figure to aim for. It was after a night of 'Snail Racing' that the total was finally achieved as two more £1,000 investors came aboard.

The last home meeting of the summer resulted in a big victory for the Tigers over Newport 60-36; four Mildenhall men had double figure with the remaining two getting nine and eight. The Fen Tigers ended the league fixtures in one of the play-off places. Robert Branford was another impressive guest for Mildenhall who were still without Heeps. A 46-44 win at the Isle of Wight made the next West Row meeting the first leg of the KO Cup against the Stoke Potters and the Soham Majorette Troup were in the stadium to entertain the crowd before the racing got underway. The start of the meeting was delayed for nearly thirty minutes as the large crowd was still making their way through the turnstiles, together with guests and visitors, plus a delegation from the Forest District Council. A tight match was expected but apart from Lambert and Sergeant, the Stoke side went down 51-43 to give the Tigers a good chance in the second-leg. Heeps was back riding once again. On the first lap in heat thirteen as Lambert seemed to move into Mildenhall's Hargreaves and all four riders collided, situation arrived with some not so good scenes but due to the quick intervention of the stewards and pit-staff it was soon quelled.

Stoke were then back at West Row in the play-off semi-final as the season moved into October. Everyone thought it was all over when the away leg was won by Mildenhall by 46-44, ending the home sides unbeaten record at Loomer Road. But the Potters soon wiped out their deficit with a 5-1 and a 3-2 in the first two heats and the match was alive once again. Mildenhall then edged their way ahead once more and were never really beaten from then on and moved into the play-off final with a 97-84 score over both legs. It is fair to say Stoke were badly hampered

-147-

by injuries when Isherwood took no more part after his first race collision, while Webster damaged his hand after rearing out of control in heat six. They were able to put only one rider in three late heats. A second half planned for this meeting was another visit from Milton Keynes and a name to look for was Connor Coles, the grandson of first Mildenhall captain and favourite Bob Coles. The Milton Keynes fans had now formed a Supporters Club with nearly fifty members, and lets not be too long in seeing a full MK Knights team in operation.

To break up the seasons thrilling finale the Bernie Klatt Memorial Trophy was brought out of hibernation for the Individual Meeting of the season. Top riders were invited and a very good line-up was seen. Riders from most of the National League were there, and it was seen that Adam Roynon was the man to beat. So it proved, and when he clashed with eventual winner Cameroon Heeps, the Dudley rider was excluded. Heeps was the winner and a run-off for second spot saw fellow Aussie Robert Branfield take runners-up place ahead of Lewis Blackbird. A fitting meeting to honour the memory of one of the founder member's of the Mildenhall Fen Tigers, the meeting was sponsored by the Klatt family of today. The brand new air fence was in place for this meeting and admired by all, but some questioned why it did not go all around the track instead of just at the ends with the bends. It was pointed out that riders riding close to the fence on the straights as they nearly always were, could be dragged into a crash if their bikes touched the air fence, so no air fence on the two straights. Former promoter Dick Partridge was one of the people behind the new fence. Once Mildenhall always Mildenhall.

Then came the final meeting of the season, and what a meeting, the second leg of the playoff final to decide who were the League Champions. Scunthorpe had built up a large lead from their home advantage. Mildenhall set about their business and seven 5-1 heat advantages and a 4-2 soon put them within striking distance. Scunthorpe came back however and when the last heat arrived the scores were as close as it could be but a 5-1 to Scunthorpe broke the Tigers fans hearts as they took the title by the margin of one point. But the Fen Tigers had completed a fantastic season under the new management and a gallant set of riders.

With the season at an end, quotes came from the riders. Cameron "I am pleased I decided to come to Mildenhall, all the boys made me welcome." Joe "It's been a pretty good season. I'm off to Australia for four months to race with Cameron." Lewis Blackbird "I had not rode since 2007 but I wanted to get back and hold down a team place and the set up at Mildenhall has helped me achieve that." What of the other riders who ended the season with Mildenhall? Jack Hargreaves proved to be an excellent choice to take over as captain, and always a team man. Lewis Blackbird's signing from Kings Lynn just before the season opened surprised many but he showed what he could really do on a speedway bike. The third rider at West Row from the start was Aaron Baseby, quickly showing his worth, and never looked back. He was joined mid-season by brother Mark who had thought about giving up the sport but gave his all for the cause during the season. Cameron Heeps was also a late starter to the season as wrangles went on with paperwork, but when he came into the team, he was a revolution to behold. Dan Halsey had been around several clubs before the management at Mildenhall saw something about him, which Dan proved with a good quality campaign as he settled in the team. The only rider back from the disastrous 2010 closure was Joe Jacobs and has turned into a firm favourite at Mildenhall as well as one of the top young riders in the League. The feel good factor was back in abundance at Mildenhall once again

****

A GLORIOUS SEASON

Success brings its problems and for the 2012 season, Mildenhall had theirs with the forty point limit, when the averages of the flourishing side of 2011 season meant they had to build virtually a new line-up. The unfortunate riders who were left out were the Baseby brothers Mark and Aaron, but a problem was solved for the Tigers when Jack Hargreaves decided to put his speedway career on hold once again, and Aaron Baseby was loaned out to the Isle of Wight. Leading the team this campaign at number one was Cameron Heeps who was doubling up with Ipswich in the Premier League, while Joe Jacobs and Lewis Blackbird were donning the Tigers colours once again, Lewis being appointed captain. Dan Halsey was also back for a second season, while a newcomer was local Brandon lad, 17 year-old Stefan Nielsen who was

(21 top) JASON GARRITY
(21 bottom) LEWIS BLACKBIRD

(22 top) JOSH BATES
(22 bottom) JOE JACOBS

**(23 top & bottom) CELEBRATIONS AT KINGS LYNN at the
PLAY-OFF SECOND LEG VICTORY**

(24) STEFAN NIELSEN number one 2013

with Scunthorpe in 2011. Extending their policy of giving youth its chance, always a Mildenhall tradition, there were two first-timers to the National League. Nathan Stoneman had decided to make the Fen Tigers his first club, and from his home in the south-west had a long journey to take each week, and Josh Bates (a Yorkshire lad) who had caught the eye in the Academy, made up the team.

The opening home meeting on 8 April was for the National Shield, which was over two legs against Dudley Heathens. The Midland club who operated from the Wolverhampton track, looked to be the favourites for the championship the coming season, led by ex Fen Tiger Adam Roynon who was also riding for Workington (Premier League) and Coventry (Elite league); yes a kink in the rules allowed this but it did seem strange at the time. Two others of their team were also doubling up with Premier teams. This match saw a bronzed Joe Jacobs, back from a winter in Australia, win the first heat of the 2012 season, and although Mildenhall were never behind they only won by one point 47-46 in a stunning first meeting. The Tiger Cubs had an outing in the second half with young riders Tyler Govier and Joe Graver, the first named coming all the way from Exeter for the chance to compete at Mildenhall.

A week later the second meeting of the season saw the Fen Tigers entertain Kings Lynn Young Stars in the National League KO Cup and they built up a fifteen point gap (55-40) for the second leg at the Norfolk Arena. The two young reserves Josh and Nathan showed they were bright prospects by following up their first meetings paid nine with another good score in the Lynn match. Cameron and Dan Halsey had two fine maximums also. Unfortunately, the second leg of the Shield at Dudley was rained off, and this after everyone had arrived and actually walked the track, plus the away meeting at Buxton and the Buxton fixture at West Row. However, the second leg of the KO Cup was run at Kings Lynn where Mildenhall won once again by twelve points to go through to the next round. 106-79. The celebrations were muted as Lewis Blackbird had received a bad shoulder injury which could keep him out for six weeks, a result of a first bend crash. Blackbird was also on the end of an alleged assault by Stars captain James Cockle after a coming together on the track; fortunately the referee saw nothing and the incident passed quickly.

Revenge for the last meeting in 2011 with Scunthorpe was achieved when they returned to West Row this season. Standing on their own this year without the help of Sheffield, meant Scunthorpe were also bringing some young riders through like the Fen Tigers. With only four heats in which a Mildenhall rider failed to score, the visitors were beaten comprehensibly 62-29, although they did lose captain Adam Wrathall following a fall in his first race. Dan Halsey was handed the captaincy with Blackbird missing and only dropped one point to the opposition.

Mildenhall was the venue for the British Youth Championships 2nd Road in May with three different classes to be run. Amongst the ten 500cc riders were a fair sprinkling of Tiger Cubs, Joining Stoneman, the reigning 500cc champions, and Bates were Joe Graver, Tyler Govier, Josh Bailey and Danny Phillips who was at Mildenhall with Scunthorpe the previous week. Mildenhall mascot Lewis Whitmore competed in the 250 class while there were fourteen very young 125 riders for the supporting races; altogether the cream of young talent. When the dust had settled it was Nathan Stoneman and Josh Bates first and second as they had in the first round at Leicester, but changing positions, while Lewis Whitmore collected seven points in his class. Nearly all these lads were 'on the books' of various speedway clubs.

The trip to the Isle of Wight was a success for the Fen Tigers and the large contingent of their supporters, when they took the points with a 49-41 scoreline. The only blip was a fall for Joe Jacobs which resulted in some severe bruising. With the bad weather intervening this was the Fen Tigers first away League fixture. Uncle Len then brought his Rye House Raiders to West Row for a meeting which is always one of the first to look for when the fixtures are published. They proceeded to surprise the Tigers and were ahead in the match until heat eight with the Tigers slow to get into gear. As it was Mildenhall avoided a shock defeat by upping their game in the second part of the meeting, but at a cost when Josh Bates injured his shoulder and would be out of action several weeks. Heeps scored a fifteen point maximum. It was also debut day for Mildenhall Academy's Joe Graver who stepped in to help out Rye House in place of their injured Tom Braddock, but after winning heat two did not trouble the scorers again. The Tiger Cubs put up a good show to win 22-12 over the Rye House Pocket Rockets, and had been fulfilling fixtures at Peterborough and Lakeside, as well as a challenge match at Coventry.

For the Rye House meeting the track staff were in action from early on the Sunday to get the track ready for speedway after the stock-cars had left it in a very difficult condition, and for the bikes it was not quite up to the usual standard. Just when most people had forgotten about the National Shield, the second leg was completed at last, resulting in the Fen Tigers first loss of the season to Dudley 52-41. They also lost Joe Jacobs with a damaged wrist. A day after a rained off meeting at West Row, the Tigers made the short journey down the A10 to bring back the points from Rye House 50-40, this being part of a double-header for the home team who took on Ipswich in the Premier League as the first taster. The Witches borrowed Dan Halsey to cover for Cameron Heeps at reserve, who was out injured while riding for Ipswich. Joe Graver made his debut for Mildenhall collecting a first ever National League win for them and a second place for his efforts.

A trip to Scunthorpe was next and a great victory by 56-35 for the Fen Tigers, but this was offset by a bad crash for teenager Nathan Stoneman who broke his left leg in a heat six crash. He actually slipped under the fence and hit a back board. This was to keep him out for the rest of the season and possibly part of the next, and just when he was beginning to show what great riding he was capable off. The great British weather was certainly playing up this year and more meetings were being called off all over the country, and even this early the fixtures were beginning to pile up, not just for Mildenhall but every club was the same.

When at last the rain held off enough to stage a Sunday meeting the visitors to West Row were the Isle of Wight led by ex-Tiger Kyle Hughes, but a comfortable win came Mildenhall's way 63-30. The Islanders did however lose Gary Cottham who fell in his second race after winning his first, and this was certainly not helped when their Dan Berwick suddenly upped and walked out of the meeting, leaving his bike behind and everyone astounded . Interesting to note five visiting riders had rode for Mildenhall early in their careers. Lewis Blackbird had guested for Leicester in the Premier League a week previous and they had offered him a place in their team which he took, but only after an agreement was reached whereby he would only miss the minimum of Tigers matches.

Mildemhall hosted the National League Best Pairs on 22 July for an afternoon with the top riders in the league. Cameron Heeps and Lewis Blackbird were the Fen Tigers representatives for this meeting. Dudley missed out when their top pair of Roynon and Ashley Morris had Premier League commitments on that day, and Stoke had Ashley Birks missing. With the points scoring changed for this competition, four points for a win, three for second and two for third it was the Tigers pairing who came out on top in the final with seventeen points, three ahead of runners-up Buxton. After coming close in the early years Mildenhall did put their name on the trophy in 1987 with Dave Jessup (10) and Mel Taylor (7) take the title for the first time

A late fight back at Buxton saw the Tigers salvage a draw and preserve their unbeaten tag in the league, but losing Josh Bates to a shoulder injury in the process. After nine heats and the Tigers twelve points adrift with steady rain falling, the track was showing pools of water. Racing continued but with one heat to go and the scores at 43-43 the meeting was abandoned but the result standing. If this was a warning the following Sunday was very wet and only a sterling effort by the track staff saw the racing commence with times well down on the normal. Visitors Stoke managed the track better and three 5-1 heat wins in the first five heats gave them an advantage they never lost, going on to smash the Fen Tigers long home record 47-45. The meeting had started off badly when the race for the Bronze Helmet saw Heeps well beaten by the holder Ashley Birks.

Mildenhall had been without their captain Blackbird for the Stoke meeting after Leicester had agreed to change times of their start to allow the Tigers to begin earlier to see him ride for both teams. Then Leicester went back to their usual start time and threatened to ban Blackbird for twenty-eight days if he didn't ride for them. The Mildenhall management were not pleased and their captain would now miss more meetings for the Fen Tigers than originally planned, as dealings between the two clubs were close to breaking point. A visit to Kings Lynn and a back to form victory54-38 as they restricted the home riders to just three heat winners. Ben Morley being a very good guest for the Tigers with double figures. New Zealander young Ryan Terry-Daley was now getting more rides in the reserve berth and a chance to show what he could do

Then came the meeting the whole of the National League was looking to when unbeaten Dudley Heathens visited West Row, this coming after a protest by the Midland club about the starting time, and wanted it to go on earlier to accommodate their top two riders who had Premier League commitments. Both teams however had to employ a guest rider. However it was the usual 4-30 start with a large group of visiting fans. With Mildenhall having the better of the racing there was an awkward moment when some of these supporters became restive and things had to be calmed down, with the help of the true Dudley followers. The Fen Tigers were the first team to lower the Heathens colours 53-36. Dudley did have their revenge two days later but as they only triumphed 54-40 the Fen Tigers were unofficial aggregate winners. Mildenhall said they were sending a protest to the BSPA and expected an apology from the Dudley management on the conduct of a small minority of their so-called supporters.

It was Stefan Nielsen's chance to grab the headlines on the visit of Stoke to West Row in the KO Cup semi-final and how(!). Stefan put on a brilliant show with six straight wins and an eighteen-point maximum. Five more wins for Blackbird gave Mildenhall a 55-39 victory and a healthy lead for the second-leg. Danish-born Stefan was also riding back home for Outrup in Denmark, with some fine performances. His form got him some rides for Ipswich. Another Tiger showing top form as the end of the season approaches was Joe Jacobs .Mildenhall went to Stoke for the National League Fours and the awesome foursome of Jacobs, Blackbird, Nielsen and Halsey sealed glory on the night to capture the Fours title to add to the Pairs. Nielsen's burst of form then saw him grab the British Under 21 championship at Sheffield, with team-mate Joe Jacobs in third place. The last home league meeting brought Kings Lynn to West Row as the Tigers wrapped up the points by 55-36, and included Aaron Baseby as a guest number one. Injuries were now beginning to bite at the line-up with Blackbird and Heeps now out of action, sustaining their injuries in Premier League action. Josh Bates was out again with a broken arm and a replacement was to be called in his place. This turned out to be Aaron Baseby who had been called back to his parent club from IOW.

Mildenhall's injury-jinx struck once again with Aaron Baseby breaking his ankle in his first match since his return to the Fen Tigers, and this after winning his first race at Stoke and third place in the next. He took a tumble into the air-fence in heat eight in the 45-45 draw, but missing the rest of the season. It was a busy week-end as the next day they took on Buxton with Mildenhall down to just five riders but the team stuck to their task and were 52-36 victors in the Trophy contest. With Heeps also out for the rest of the season Mildenhall were bringing in Jason Garrity as a guest number one for as many meetings as possible, the Rye House man was proving a hit with the Fen Tigers fans, and he was enjoying his outings at West Row, and had become a 'adopted' Fen Tiger. As well as his startling style on the track he was setting to and helping out as much in the pits.

To try and strengthen the lower order Mildenhall obtained the services of Gareth Isherwood the former Stoke rider who had been out of action with broken bones in his back for nearly a year. He made his debut at Stoke and then at West Row against Buxton. The latter meeting chalked up a big 60-30 win as the Hitmen managed just two heat winners. The National League Riders Championship continued to elude Mildenahll although they had three of their riders in the final at Rye House on 29 September. Nielsen, Blackbird and Jacobs however did not show anything like their best and finished down the field, although Stefan and Lewis did mange one heat win each as Ashley Birks took the honours.

The National Trophy was taking shape but postponed meetings because of the weather was doing its best to prevent these meetings from taking place, and the teams involved were kept busy fitting these matches in. Mildenhall had lost their first meeting in the Trophy at the Isle of Wight but were still in with a good chance as the other three teams began to take points off each other. When the Trophy fixture with IOW was wiped out by the weather it was hastily arranged for the following week when the Islanders were due at West Row for the Play-off semi-final. This turned into a double-header with the Fen Tigers victors in both matches, Stefan Nielsen, or 'rubber man' as some had named him, walked away from another frightening crash in the second match.

Along came Dudley Heathens once again to West Row, this time for the National League KO Cup Final (1st leg). Cameron Heeps had been confirmed as missing for the remainder of the fixtures, so super-sub Garrity was seen as the key to the rest of the season, if he was always available. Against the Heathens Mildenhall put on one of their best displays of the season to reduce Dudley to a 61-33 defeat, and who had to wait until heat eight to record their first heat advantage. They did however lose captain Byron Bekker with a dramatic crash in his first outing, and was rushed straight to hospital, but with everyone hoping it was not so bad as it looked at the time. Joe Haines and Tom Perry with double figures tried to rescue something for Dudley but their back-up strength was not up to the task, Mildenhall taking a lead of twenty-eight to the away leg. Josh Bates had made a surprising come-back in place of Isherwood with great results totalling a paid twelve. This then became the basis for a Dudley protest, another in a season long feud between the two clubs. Having named Isherwood as a replacement for Bates, the Dudley promoter argued he was not eligible and his points should be taken off the score. Mildenhall however had received permission to bring him back in for Isherwood it he recovered enough from his broken arm, and the protest was dismissed.

Yet another injury struck Mildenhall on the run-in of the season. Lewis Blackbird sustained a broken collar-bone riding for Leicester at Newcastle and looked to be out until next year. Effects and days were getting tighter to get the meetings on before the deadline of 31 October, and this was not helped when the West Row meeting versus Stoke in the Trophy was called off after five heats when the rain came down in 'buckets'. This was quickly re-arranged for the last day of the season. Meanwhile a Tuesday night at Monmore Green saw Mildenhall face Dudley twice in one evening first for the Play-off Final (1st leg) and then the second leg of the KO Cup. The Fen Tigers held on to their Cup lead as the match was abandoned after twelve heats, the score standing as the Tigers had a winning lead to retain the KO Cup. The first clash between the sides had left Mildenhall to overcome the Dudley lead of fourteen points to claim the league title. The second leg of the Play-off final had to be moved to Kings Lynn the very next night as the West Row track was under water, but the Mildenhall supporters travelled in their hundreds to the Norfolk Area.

After a long wait in the rain while the Lynn track staff done a wonderful job in getting the circuit ready for the meeting to go on, Mildenhall also saw the Dudley favourite Adam Roynon back in their line-up for this encounter. A few tricky heats and the wet track became steadily quicker and the Fen Tigers flourished although Roynon was top dog in the early heats. Lewis Blackbird made a dramatic come-back to everyone's amazement but showed nothing of his injury as he, with the rest of a hard riding Mildenhall team proceeded to cut the lead down and then went ahead. A last heat horrifying crash between Stefan Nielsen and Roynon saw the Dudley rider excluded, and nursing a broken leg. The Tigers then shared the last heat to become National League Champions once again, and how the supporters celebrated. News came of another complaint being put in by Dudley that Chris Louis of the Mildenhall promotion had influenced the referee when he was viewing the video tape in his last heat decision to exclude the Dudley rider. This was soon discarded and the Fen Tigers took the crown.

At home to Stoke, the final meeting of the season at West Row was completed before the rain decided to come back again. Mildenhall won to make their haul for the 2012 season five trophies, a record that no-one could see ever being achieved before, this included the Fours and the Pairs, also being voted top sporting team in Suffolk. The last night of the season ended in a packed clubroom and bar to see the trophies on display, plus the Bronze Helmet in the hands of Stefan Nielsen, and then the champers flowed.

****